HEALING IS REQUIRED

THE JOURNEY TO TRUTH, WISDOM,
AND THE HEART OF HEALING

Anika Apple

Memoir Disclaimer

While this book is not a memoir, it does contain personal historical events. The events and experiences shared in Healing Is Required are true to the best of my memory and recollection. They are presented as I experienced and understood them at the time. However, memory is imperfect, and perspectives differ. Not all family members, friends, or individuals mentioned were aware of these events as they unfolded, and their own recollections may vary, especially if their interactions with the people and situations described were different from mine. This book is not intended to cause harm, misrepresent, or disparage anyone. Any resemblance to specific individuals outside of my own lived experience is purely coincidental.

This book is a deeply personal account, and while I have taken care to be truthful, it is ultimately my story as I lived it. Names and certain details may have been changed for privacy and clarity.

Advice Disclaimer

The insights and guidance shared in Healing Is Required are based on my personal experiences and what has worked for me. I am not a licensed therapist, psychologist, or medical professional, and nothing in this book should be taken as medical, psychological, or professional advice. Readers should use their own judgement and seek appropriate professional support when needed.

Any progress, growth, or transformation a reader experiences will depend on their own unique circumstances, efforts, and actions. I cannot guarantee specific outcomes, as every individual's journey is different. This book is meant to inspire and empower, not to serve as a substitute for professional help or guidance.

HEALING IS REQUIRED

Dedication

For Adrian Jr and Aniya- May your life be full of the healing power of wonder. May your compass be your relationship with our Source, God. May curiosity be fuel for your mind and body. May your love for humanity be contagious. May your light be witnessed and received by all who have the honor of encountering you. May God be glorified in all you do. May you feel my love for you each day. Thank you for witnessing my healing and embracing your own.

For George and Deanna- without you, there simply is no me as I exist today. Thank you for all of who you are and for giving me space for my growth. Loving you is healing to my soul.

For Vichi- our friendship and sisterhood have transformed me for decades. Your words have helped me heal from moments I didn't think I would survive. I am so grateful for your wisdom and love.

For Deborah- God chose you to be a pillar in my life and knew that I would need your love and guidance. Thank you for seeing my heart and reflecting God's promises and wisdom to me in the way that only you can. You are a walking reminder of God's miracles in so many ways. I love you so deeply.

For Leilani, Kailei, Josette, Miriam, Myra, and Deanna (my precious earthly mother), your healing inspires us all. Thank you for creating the playground for me to test and learn as the world of healing unfolds. You are a precious part of this work.

And...

The Collective Community- Earth Angels, Lightworkers, Divine Healers, International Marketplace Mavens Movement, The Healing Crusade and the remnant.

May this healing narrative remind you of your core purpose and propel you into action. May it remind you that you are capable and worthy. You are the miracle. You are the change. You are the answer.

Peace and Blessings,

Anika Apple

Contents

Foreward

"Healing is the return of the memory of wholeness."

- Deepak Chopra

We can all look around us and see that we, as a human collective, are not well. Divisiveness, war, violence, rage, famine, oppression, and the erosion of humanity are not root causes–they are symptoms. They reveal our deep wounding and our urgent need to return to greater connection, expanded consciousness, and most of all–healing. That's why this book is so important.

Throughout the pages of this book, clearly channeled from the Divine, Anika Apple calls us up and in. Her words stir our spirits, reminding us of what is possible: to be whole, connected, and healed human beings. Her words penetrate. They confront us. They linger in our hearts, urging us to not stay stagnant, but instead to *become*. To become better, greater, and more beautiful versions of ourselves.

Because when we heal, the world heals.

The timing of this book could not be more meaningful. We are living in an urgent moment. Governments are displacing and discarding people as though they are objects. Leaders are choosing greed and power over compassion and dignity. The toll on our mental, emotional, physical, and spiritual health is undeniable.

The "us" versus "them" mentality that is prevalent throughout the world is ripping societies apart. The decline is grave. And the remedy is clear: healing. From all of us.

Over the years, I have worked with thousands of individuals through my coaching and leadership development practice. Early on, I realized I could help leaders *look* the part, *act* the part, even *play* the part of strong leadership. But if they were not right within – if they had not done the inner work to build a strong foundation–

Healing Is Required is the blueprint to help us all heal from within. It shows us how to reclaim our wholeness, take control of our lives, and lay the foundation for becoming the extraordinary humans we were created to be.

The choice is ours. And the impact is–

— *Kailei Carr, CEO & Founder, The Asbury Group*

Preface

There are moments in life that are pivotal in nature. Special moments that help to shape the foundation of human existence. Moments where inspiration meets intention and change occurs. Moments when faith is deepened and miracles are witnessed. This book marks a moment in the history of the world. It presents a clear decision point that will impact the soul's journey of humanity. It is a call to action and a reminder of who you are at your core. It is a revelry of faith. It is a precious gift from above, calling you into truth and purpose.

This book marks the moment humanity needs. The heart of mankind desires change—a return to truth and a genuine awakening of the world's collective consciousness.

As the human author of this work, I have been blown away by the brilliance of the "downloads" that I have received about the journey to help humanity heal. As I was writing, I would tell people, "I am writing two books at the same time. One is God's, and the other is mine." This book belongs to "us," to humanity, but make no mistake: this book is God's. I, like many divinely led authors, have written the book, but it came directly from God.

The words you read and how they transform your mind are the work of the divine. The miracles you experience as you explore the concepts in action result from God's words resonating in your heart. This book is an avenue to reconnect you with the truth of your own divinity and to inspire you to seek God's truth on your own.

I wrote this book relatively quickly as it was downloaded to me. I would pray and then sit at my laptop, watching as the words filled the pages. Every story recounted was in divine agreement with God. God would bring back memories and images while I was writing to deepen my connection to the concepts and vision shared in the book. The work described on the pages that follow very intentionally calls you into your healing work because it is required. We are very close to a tipping point, and the more collective movement to heal that occurs, the more glory we will experience in this lifetime. That is why this book matters. Simply put, it is required.

I have been on a journey with God my entire life. During my childhood, I encountered a variety of experiences. I am a survivor of sexual trauma, domestic violence, grief, depression, and anxiety, all of which happened amidst a remarkable life. While I was experiencing sexual trauma as a young child, I knew that the only way I would be able to address it was with the strength that came from God. I gave my life to God when I was about nine years old. I floated down the aisle in the church. It was as if my body knew I was returning home to my first parent, the one who I knew could see what was happening to me and could fix it without a word on my part.

The same sentiment is true for me at the time of writing this book. My heart knows that the love of God is the only way we can address the ills of the world and our own human depravity and begin the path to healing. God has graced me with an incredible gift to create peace in environments, see into the hearts of others, and help people heal. It is an honor and an assignment that I take incredibly seriously. It is my calling. It is my love.

In the heart of the pandemic, I met a man through a course that I was taking. He shared with the group that he had done some work on his profile, which interested me. A few days prior, a close friend asked if I knew anyone who could do the profile work this man described. Of course, I reached out to the man. We had a 20-minute call planned. I prepared three questions and an intro that was two minutes long to ensure we could maximize the time.

Over an hour later, I was scouring the page of notes before me, my mind absolutely blown by the experience. After my intro, I asked him to tell me a bit more about himself and his journey. He began to share so many fascinating things about his life. Then it happened. He told me, "Anika, you are going to heal the world." I find it remarkable that I was able to keep jotting down notes while he continued talking. I was listening. I was writing. My mind, however, was going back to my prayer time several weeks ago when God said to me, "I have sent you to heal the world." I never told a soul, not a single person. I never even said it aloud to myself, lest the mere utterance of it create some kind of spiritual backlash or friction with my Christian upbringing. Of course, one person- a mere human- could not heal the world.

Or could they? Heal the world, that is. I remember sitting for a long time after that conversation. Of course, I will heal the world. I mean, we will heal the world together. It is the power of God working through any of us that allows our purpose to be experienced in the world. Mine happens to be deeply focused on exposing divine truths, helping people see themselves, and ushering forth God's love, which is the ultimate pathway to healing. My work is to galvanize others to do their part, which will continue the beautiful healing work we need to heal the world.

This may seem controversial to you. Perhaps even with a bit of ego. "She thinks that she is going to heal the world?" Yes. In fact, I know that it will happen. God will heal the world, and "we," those committed to being in our purpose, will be conduits for the world's healing. I had to say yes. I had to believe. I had to seek God and surrender. I had to let go of the magnitude of the statement about my healing the world and the intense fear I felt in order to say yes. When I let go of the fear, I remembered it was God's work and plan. Surrendering took time, a lot of time. I had to do my own healing work to accept what God says about me. Trust me, everything you might be thinking in relation to "healing the world," I've already thought for you. I wrestled, and God won. What is God's will is already done.

"So what happens to the people that don't choose to heal?" "What if people read the book but are not compelled to shift their perspective?" I don't know, but God does. It is God's plan. My sharing of this story is a direct result of God's guidance. For many of you reading this, it will encourage you to stand in the truth of what God says about you and who you know you are. We have to be bold enough to believe in God. I believe God is going to heal the world, and that all the other people called to do so will deepen our faith and come together in ways that are monumental. That is what I believe. How and when is not my business. I will wait patiently for God's timing, and in the meantime, I will continue to call others forward into their purpose and the recognition that our choices matter.

Hi. I am Anika Apple—a precious child of God. I have a divine assignment that involves helping you connect more deeply with your truth and God. I am here to help us heal. This book belongs to God. I am simply the vessel given the honor of writing it and doing my human best to express God's love for you, for all of us. I carry a special heart for God. I look forward to whatever God reveals to you in your own time with them and to witnessing your shifts as you digest this book.

The Truth Is Required

Our collective and individual healing is so critical at this time that we had to be the recipients of this book, which calls our attention to the fact that healing is required. Reflect for a moment on a movie or show where a character has been wounded but is unaware. The body works quickly, releasing endorphins, which enable the person to keep going. The character may keep moving to escape inherent danger without recognizing that another dangerous condition is worsening inside them. They may bleed on others without knowing. They might begin to notice other symptoms arising and attempt to address them without taking care of the initial issue. That is where we are. The wounds we don't see, have forgotten, or long ignored are still pervasive and threaten our existence. They cannot be solved by hoping for improvement or by averting our eyes from the gaping holes in our bodies. Healing is required; to heal, we must begin by seeing the truth from a different vantage point.

This book is divinely written. It is the genuine desire from above that we heal. The intentionality of words, the examples, and the countless points of inflection are precisely placed to help you see humanity's collective condition. The work is both inspired and directed by the Divine's love for us, their precious creation. They desire that we might achieve our highest potential in life, which requires our commitment to healing and evolving.

Healing has become a buzzword. It is missing the inherent messages of depth, self-love, and mental elevation that were once foundational and almost synonymous with the term. This is a concern for all of us, because it is healing that we seek. We are often misled into believing that it is an event rather than an ongoing journey and the unlocking of our highest potential.

All too often, we water down the meaning of words. Shifting the meaning may not be intentional, but the dilution tends to erode the real meaning. People often discuss healing in a way that lacks substance. Stating that "you need to heal" significantly understates the criticality of healing. Healing is complex and deep work. It requires being open to experiencing your truth in ways you haven't been able to. Your frame of reference is constantly evolving, creating the opportunity to see yourself in a different light. Introspection needs grace as its companion. Self-love, forgiveness, and grace for yourself are not as readily taught by societies that benefit from self-sacrificing tendencies.

This Is Big Work! The encouraging part is that you can do it. You were made to do it. Throughout this book, you will come into contact with many truths that will help you explore and seek even more wisdom. That wisdom will help you heal. It will spark your curiosity and encourage you to keep digging. By cultivating a loving relationship with yourself, one filled with grace and a desire to understand, you will recognize that you are capable. You are meant to do this work. Your healing journey will create freedom within yourself that you have only dreamed about. It is amazing. It is also a journey. The path has many twists and turns, and to be honest, it is not always easy.

It is worth it. Healing, that is. It matters to you and the collective in ways you have not yet considered. As an individual, the healing work that you do helps you understand and accept your purpose. You can only reach your highest potential by addressing areas that need healing. It may help you to think of healing as the pathway to your highest self.

Healing plays a crucial role in advancing societies. If you consider the amount of distrust and unrest that exists in countries around the world, you will find that much of the impact is rooted in violence and inequality. Without addressing the inherent truth about how societies have been built, many through domineering power, theft, and dishonesty, it is no surprise that deep-rooted injustices persist that have not been healed. Truth and reconciliation are crucial components in the healing journey. The missing piece is the genuine acknowledgement of injustice or other conditions that caused the impact. The risk is massive- it will continue to disrupt peace and abundance. Adversarial systems lack inherent mechanisms that facilitate the healing of underlying differences. Monarchical systems require acquiescence from their people. It is not necessarily a system flaw, but there is an assumption that people will accept and move forward. There will always be unrest in any relationship, with perpetual advantages given to one side. The solution lies in healing, which occurs at both the individual and collective levels.

As you read this, you are beginning to wonder if there is a correlation between healing and potential. It is so. Healing is required. The wounds we have sustained on this journey and that we carry with us into our human existence are the most significant barriers to our highest potential; they stymie our ascent to a purpose-filled life. As the categorization of what "healing" is becomes oversaturated with notions, potions, and oceans of fad-frenzy rhetoric, it's not difficult to understand why people do not see healing clearly. This book is the beginning of the foundational journey you need to take to heal yourself.

This book is not about me; it is about us—the collective. We need healing. We are inter-connected or, as I liked to say in my youth, "inexplicably tied" together. We are one people. Well, of course, we are. Fish are fish. They all inhabit the same environment- that of water. There are many different types of fish, and the water conditions vary, but they share waters that extend from one part of the Earth to another. Their environment impacts them, and they, in turn, impact that same environment. Overcrowding, pollution, drought, and global warming are all factors that affect all fish; how they migrate impacts habitat, temperature, reproduction, and their ability to thrive.

We can easily see the parallels by applying the same concepts to humanity. We are all impacted by our environment. We all impact our environment. This means that we are tied together. In the same way that the fish are connected by their habitat, we are connected by ours. The choices that we make around our environment impact all of us. Consider the impacts of global warming and its far-reaching effects. Pandemics and choices about how to protect communities from threats have a broad-based impact. We cannot ignore the truth that we are connected. For many, this mere fact creates a sense of purpose. For some, it creates a massive amount of discomfort. For others, the disconnect may go far beyond discomfort. Our experiences, as well as the generational wounds we have carried into this lifetime, can breed distrust in others. That creates a significant issue. ***The distrust that often exists between people hinders our ability to accept that we are indeed one people.*** That is a fact. We have a choice. That is also a fact.

Much of humanity has decided that rather than extending choice to everyone, manipulation is the way to hold onto control. It is a way to influence behavior, but it is not in the best interest of all. It is self-serving and destructive. The desire to control is rooted in fear. A fundamental disconnect exists here. Control would only be required if there were no possible way that the alternative could create an acceptable outcome. If left to individual choice, wouldn't people naturally choose what is "best?" The fear that another person will choose something that is not aligned with the desired outcome lies at the heart of the desire for control. This is aligned with a scarcity mindset and oppressive behavior. Both have roots in unhealed conditions within the person. This can also be observed in group behavior. The unhealed conditions in one are recognized by another. Circumstances can either draw people together or repel them. This provides additional evidence that a connection exists between people. The connection to each other is complex and clearly exacerbated by unhealed conditions and the absence of a clear picture of what is best for the collective.

The people who are being oppressed by these mindsets are at the greatest risk of living unhealed lives. The truth is shrouded from them. They have tucked away much of their ability to question and discern truth. This is not due to a lack of desire or interest. It is simply connected to the unhealed conditions that have become unnoticeable to the inhabitants of their human vessel.

These truths will be unpacked as we journey together. This book is not merely informational; it is intended to be transformational. ***Healing is required, and this is a call to action.***

This book is intended to spark thought, illuminate healthy tension within you, and challenge the current paradigms around you. You can expect numerous questions to arise. You might be wondering about where this book will take you, which is to be expected. Be aware that many of the questions you have will expand as you read. The questions might start small and grow vast as you expand your awareness to accept more possibilities. Some questions will have suitable answers on these pages. Many of the thoughts that arise for you will require your own meditation and prayer time. You should expect to receive a revelation that supports the level of knowledge you need at this moment. Other questions will remain unanswered because the moment for that information has not yet been determined.

This is an excellent book for your book club, prayer circle, family reading, and religious/spiritual organization to experience together. Simply stated, by reading together, you will expand your minds together. Your perspective will begin to shift as you discuss concepts, share your stories, and begin to heal together. This book is flowing through me so that you can make a conscious decision to see yourself, own your unhealed self, and choose to see yourself as worthy of being healed. At the next level, you will also realize that your decision to heal or not impacts the entire collective, not just your family unit. The call to action is simple- Will you choose to heal yourself to facilitate the healing required for humanity to thrive?

Chapter Pearls

- Healing is individual and collective work.

- Healing is the pathway to reaching the highest potential in each person.

- Unhealed conditions are at the center of fear-based behavior. Identifying them can create connections with others who have similar wounds or repel them.

- Humanity is connected. Individual healing, or the lack thereof, impacts the collective as a whole.

Journal Prompts

How has healing shaped your experience to date?

What sparked your curiosity to read this book, and why? What do you hope to find within the pages, and how might it support you on your journey?

What examples of unhealed conditions and their impact are you experiencing (or have experienced), and how has it impacted your life?

What collective behaviors do you believe are connected to unhealed conditions and why?

What is the biggest obstacle to your healing journey? What thoughts are starting to form that might help you heal?

How to Use This Book

This book is divided into three parts to guide you through the process of healing:

Part One: The Awakening helps you see with new eyes.

Part Two: The Deep Work invites you into soul-level transformation.

Part Three: The Return shows you how to live out your healing with God, in community, and on purpose.

Each chapter includes **Chapter Pearls** (core truths) and **Journal Prompts** to help you process and integrate what you're discovering. Return to these as often as needed. Some truths will land right away; others may deepen over time.

Healing isn't linear. Don't worry about rushing forward or "getting it right." The structure offers a map, but your spirit will guide you to the places that need light.

Come as you are. The invitation is always open.

Chapter One

The Call

There is a moment that exists before you "know" something. The moment you make an assumption based on the context and perspective of the current circumstances. That moment shifts when you receive sufficient knowledge to create a new understanding. We process information through our experiences, requiring us to use our minds. The mind is conditioned to create a sense of safety for us. If new information somewhat threatens our current truths, some friction will arise. The discomfort of friction is often the basis for choosing not to embrace new information. This is a harmful practice. Expanding our perspective is increasingly crucial for humanity. The broader your frame of reference, the stronger your capacity to make solid, well-thought-out decisions.

It is easy to discount what you have never experienced or seen. Perhaps it is too easy even to pretend that unseen situations don't exist. We might believe that something we have never seen cannot possibly be real. How can that be if others have seen and experienced it? Consider the number of people who have encountered Bigfoot, the Loch Ness monster, or even alternative life forms. Whether you believe in their existence is not the point. What matters is that you made a choice to believe in it or not, even as you read the sentence.

"Oh, I don't believe that Bigfoot exists."

"There is no such thing as the Loch Ness Monster."

"I know my aunt saw that lifeform she described, even though I didn't see it myself."

Regardless of your opinion about those examples, you have most likely made a choice. That is the point here. Agreement, disagreement, or choosing indifference are all choices. All too often, the fact that a choice is before you is overlooked. Perhaps you have never personally experienced any of the aforementioned phenomena. You can still decide it is possible until you have collected sufficient evidence for the alternative. If you decide their existence is not possible, you shut the door to the prospect that it could be true. Once you close off possibilities, your seeking ends. Indifference is a choice as well. No choice is the same as choosing that it is not plausible that they could exist.

This is a crucial concept to grasp as you read this book. You will be presented with truths that you may not recognize or have experienced yet in this life. Openness to possibilities will help you connect with what is presented here in your own base of truth. For so many of you, your experience will be one of resonance and even remembering. For others, it will be an awakening. Allow your posture to be one of being open to possibilities. You will deeply benefit from it.

You will have a choice as you absorb what is presented in the book. You will not be the same, even if you disagree with the truths shared in each chapter. You will have to decide what to believe, explore, and what to do with the information that you have read. Note that even choosing not to make a decision is a choice. Once you have knowledge, to turn away from it is to deny it. There is intentionality in denying information that does not exist before we actually know it. It means that once you read the truths in this book, you have a decision to make.

Your choices will impact your life and the lives of those in your lineage. This is also a divine fact. Your decision impacts the environment. Think, "I can either create or dissolve the energy that propels humanity toward the healing required for us to thrive." The collective decisions will have an impact that extends beyond the current generation.

For much of our existence, "thriving" represented an experience that had not felt attainable by most. That sentiment is correct. There is a wide variety of experiences around the world that people can recount. Thriving is not experienced by all at any level of wealth, social status, or other characteristics. Regardless of the varying socio-economic conditions, people's experience of "thriving" is varied. **The key element to thriving is healing**. Of course, it remains true that the other conditions must improve in order to experience life as intended. Access to resources can be significantly improved. Wealth is so often used as a weapon to minimize and even oppress others. Social structures, designed as a sign of times far past, have outstretched the need of the moment and have morphed into what some believe are their birthrights. Most of what we consider the current social structure today is out of order and will require genuine truth and reconciliation for healing and restoration to take place.

Those who have committed to supporting the healing of the collective will continue to rise in places of influence and impact. Unfortunately, for many others in power today, this means they will not maintain their powerful perch. They are being uprooted and will continue to be so as long as they do not encourage, support, and facilitate the required collective healing. The road is not easy, but it is required.

This is the most significant shift humanity has ever and likely will ever experience. Why 'likely,' you might ask. Simply put, we have the answers required for this moment and have been given the opportunity to see and understand. The wisdom you possess and its ability to help humanity connect with its internal truth are incredibly potent. As the truth about choice is recognized, you take an active role in developing what is to come. It is impossible to be genuinely passive when you have sufficient knowledge to make an informed decision. You are actively choosing to act on or ignore the truth. Collectively, more is known than ever before, and our healing will open the door even further.

It would be an error of judgement to assume that we have a complete understanding of everything. Humanity will benefit from taking the time to digest what is currently known, including making choices in a more conscious state. We will be more apt to embrace new truths as they are revealed when we encounter them in a state of healing. Even if we received a divine blueprint of the times beyond this moment, we would still not fully understand it. The Divine, in Their wisdom, provides what we need for the moment. As we progress, it is essential to note that the word 'moment' is not limited to how humanity perceives time. It is an expansive term, and the most straightforward way to understand how God looks at time.

It is true that for years, some of humanity has thrived. Some people possess extraordinary wealth, power, and influence; perhaps this is the image that comes to mind when you think about abundance. In a healed condition, there is a recognition that, as part of the collective, one has a responsibility to teach and support others. For many, one of their unhealed conditions is that of greed. Greed is connected to a scarcity mindset and rooted in fear, even though you may see confidence as the leading characteristic of those who come to mind.

We have more than enough resources, wisdom, and human energy to address any issue we experience in the world. While the masses continue to operate in this unhealed state, others have begun healing and are working towards the collective shift. Many have seized the opportunity and are enjoying their seat of power, unaware of the irreparable damage being done to humanity. The remaining group completely understands what is at risk for them when we begin the healing process. It stands to reason that those in power want to maintain their position. The ego is being fed; rewards are coming in for the risks taken to reach this point, and they see no need to look at the unhealed conditions within.

Essentially, they are not being challenged by the masses. It would be difficult for the masses to challenge the unhealed conditions of those in power when they have not healed themselves. We cannot yield the collective authority given to us by the Divine when we are unhealed. *We are the generators of our own fear.* That fear sits within us, reminding us that we are not healed, we are incomplete, and therefore, unworthy of more. This narrative exists within anyone who will allow it to remain. The way to fully eradicate it is through healing. Affirmations, self-help books, coaching, energy work, and the lotions, potions, and motions peddled on the internet will not do it alone. True healing is required.

Many of the aforementioned can be resources for you during your journey, and most are genuinely additive. It is essential to acknowledge that even more resources are required. Most of the tactics that exist are missing two fundamentals: 1- You are the COO of your life, which includes your healing process, and therefore, you must co-create it with the CEO and bring the operational strategy to life. You are accountable for the operations and integration of the healing. 2- You cannot heal without God. While you are created with an innate ability to heal yourself, God is essential for complete healing. We'll explore this profound concept in greater depth in the upcoming chapters.

A Word about God...

When faced with challenges, it's only natural for our ego to want us to shut down or give up. Right now, it might be screaming for you to "close the book" and walk away. Instead, choose to tell the ego that you are shifting to a focus on your healing, and therefore, it needs to recognize that you are safe and that the concepts you will read herein support your health and well-being. That will help you calm your well-equipped 'fight or flight' response, addressing your nervous system. Take a deep breath and keep reading. You deserve to have the information necessary to live your best life. That means you must confront some difficult truths, whether in this book or out in the world.

People in your inner circle who have started their healing work may be able to offer support to you. Or, you may be the trailblazer in your circle and have no one else to process this with (hence the resources outlined in the book.. Either way, God is the support you need and is always available.

Notice the order of the fundamentals. *Why is God second?* For many who are religious, listing God second is out of order. God recognizes the limitations of the human mind and the separation we see from Them. The order specifically addresses you as the COO first because our immediate reaction is to look inward first. Part of healing is to be aware of oneself, which includes perceived limitations. The perception of limitations will be discussed throughout this book. For now, you can choose to remain open to receive what is for you in this book. The best way to do that is to understand your role first and then accept God's part in your life, specifically your healing.

God is at the center of healing. *All healing comes from God.* You can comprehend and accept this as fact. God is expansive, much more than the human mind can understand. In simple terms, let us clarify that in this book (and hopefully in life), you accept the name 'God' as the representation of your higher power. For those who believe and look to their higher self, consider the expansiveness of the self as a part of God. Let us not waste time wrestling with terminology in an effort to prop up religious affiliations or to pit beliefs against each other. There is a time for religious and spiritual discourse, but this is not it. The name "God" will be used throughout the book (interchangeable with "The Divine" and "Source") as these are the terms God directs us to use in this book. They are one and the same. Be encouraged in this moment to release the tension you have around your desire to define God differently. Notice yourself at this moment. Where is the tension coming from? Is it ego? The desire to be right? Fear of challenging your upbringing? To create a sense of things by placing a box around them to make it make sense? Please assure yourself that it is okay. The probing questions are here simply because that is how most people will and are responding to this moment. It is okay. Hold fast to the truth that it is ok not to know or fully understand everything. You are expansive enough to accept that two things can be true simultaneously. We will explore both of these truths throughout the book.

Now that God is conceptually established and we have aligned on the name, let's return to God's role in our lives. We co-create our lives with God. Long before we were born, God had a plan for our lives. For some religions, this is a foundational principle. For others, it is a contradictory concept. At the core, though, we can agree that there is a purpose for all of us, and there is a plan to deliver purpose. The plan may be very loose and constantly evolving, but there is some level of this concept that we can accept.

We are the co-authors of this plan with God. Before we were born, before coming to the human vessel, we designed this path with God. In our humanness, God reminds us that we have a choice. The choice is essentially the continued extension of the co-authoring of our lives that began before we were born. You have likely had the fleeting thought, "I would not have chosen…" and then listed several situations you believe you would not have accepted. At this moment, hold on to the truth that because you could see more of your life, the possibilities, and how your life intersected with the collective (ultimately into God's divine plan), you said yes. You understood more about the path at that moment than you have access to now.

What is meant by "access"? This refers to the act of remembering what you knew before birth or tapping into your ever-present knowing. At this moment, you may want to pause your reading to write in your journal. All of the emotions flowing through you now are very important. Capture the essence of the feelings and thoughts without judgement as you notice them. They don't require judgement. No one is interested in judgement. The only thing needed at this moment is to see and accept that, regardless of your path thus far, you said "Yes" to the divine mission. Trust yourself. Trust God.

It may be helpful to take time to reflect. Think of a moment you had to do something that you knew would be incredibly difficult. You likely created a plan that outlined every controllable detail. The process of constructing a house is a great example. You see the beginning and the end. You may not know how all of the pieces will fall exactly into place, but you know there is a plan, and you trust that you have enough instructions and information to ensure that there is a house at the end of the work you are putting forth. That is this moment. You had enough information to say yes. You believed that this work, your purpose, was important enough to say yes to. You knew that because of the experiences you would have up to this point, you would be the best person for the work that you and God designed. Breathe into it. It is another divine truth. It is also evidence of your worthiness and bravery. Take some time to write in your journal. This is a moment where healing exists.

Now that we have established that there is a divine plan and that we have a role in it, we can accept that there is a CEO. Unlike some of the less favorable examples of CEOs portrayed in the media, many are mission-focused or purpose-led. They know that co-creating strategies, vision, and purpose is required to ensure sustainability and suitability for the organizations they lead. They recognize that as an individual, they cannot possibly represent the organization's broad range of thoughts and ideas, so they have brilliant, trusted advisors who co-create the way forward.

This is an important distinction to highlight. They are often portrayed as disconnected and even disinterested in the masses. It may be true for some, but that does not make it universally true. You can choose to consider it a privilege to be in a position to extend grace to another person who is also in need of healing. Their roles as CEOs are often misunderstood and can be quite lonely. They see and know a lot about the things that are going wrong or creating risk in the business, and they have come to terms with the fact that they will have to accept the blame, even for things they tried to avoid or warn against.

Does this sound a little like the role of the Divine in our lives? God wants the best for us and yet holds the blame the moment things go differently than we wanted, even when we did not do what we were supposed to. The overarching responsibility is God's; therefore, God is our CEO. It does not mean that it is God's fault or that everything happens because of God. Our unhealed condition

All Healing Comes From God

Healing comes from God and is generated within you. We make healing sound complicated and complex, but it is relatively simple. Healing is love. It is the process of applying a salve, like love, acceptance, or forgiveness. It is the process of designing a unique poultice, combined with all of the necessary herbs and oils, packed with the power to reach the issue's core. The poultice has everything it takes to treat the root of the issue, not simply ease symptoms. It is applying faith in your ability to heal yourself with your inner guidance.

Traditional medication can be used to support healing. There is a role for medication, but nothing outweighs the mindset of a human who believes in their ability to heal. Sometimes, the belief is placed in medication, a healer, or a natural remedy. Decades of research about placebos prove that the mind can be powerful enough to create the same improvement as those receiving the treatment. The wisdom we should take from this is that if we learn to use our mind in alignment with the source of our inner wisdom, God, we can heal ourselves.

If that is the case, you may ask why so many people are sick. Why hasn't my condition healed? Why has my condition returned? This is what makes healing so complicated. The Human Condition is what gets in the way. Notice how the questions here and those that arose in your mind are likely accusatory and outwardly focused.

The question we would benefit from asking starts with ourselves. What is it about what I am doing that may keep me in suffering? How is what I am doing not facilitating my healing? How can I learn from my experiences so that I can effectively teach others? Is there anything that I am doing inconsistently that may be contributing to the demise of my health? The human condition is at the core of our thought patterns.

In the next chapter, we will delve into perspective and dissect how we think in order to create even more insight and moments of introspection for you. At this moment, hold the truth that our ego, which is very good at its job, often starts from a belief that our human self can do no wrong. Even those who usually wrestle with lower self-esteem can relate to the ego's initial positioning of "It cannot be me."

The beauty of this moment is that you can release any tension about your humanness getting in the way. It is not your fault. **In fact, there is no benefit in ever looking for fault.** That is a distraction that keeps our minds from focusing on what is and what is not. Choose to accept that you are learning about your ability to do and be more than you realized was possible.

Accepting the knowledge that you are expanding at this moment will support your inner being in relaxing. As the tension melts away, you are invited to laugh or smile. Yes, you are relaxed now because you have removed the feeling of guilt for not knowing what you didn't know. The mind creates an interesting cycle for us. **The beauty of things is that you can unwind the patterns and choose to accept divine truth instead of limiting thinking.**

How do you feel at this moment? This would be a good time to journal).Your experience as you read the last two paragraphs was likely transformative, even if you don't realize it yet. If you have continued to read, even with a skeptical mindset, you have expanded your perspective to a place of possibilities. This is where healing can begin! If you allowed the thoughts to connect for you as intended, you experienced the 'lightbulb' moment. You were able to make the connection even though it felt unfamiliar and uncomfortable. This is growth, and you can celebrate.

Our lives are spent in moments where our systems work overtime to keep us safe. The body is brilliant and wonderfully made. As the race to protect us unfolds, we must allow ourselves to accept the new information. Again, you are witnessing the power of the mind. It can control the system designed to protect you. Communicating with the limbic system, which is responsible for "fight or flight," your mind can allow the system to access the information that you need.

This is also how healing takes place. Your body becomes conditioned in a familiar state. That state may be one of dis-ease. The state now becomes what your body wants to protect. It aims to foster a symbiotic relationship between your natural state and the state induced by the dis-ease. The desire to return to homeostasis is the driving factor, even if the body must accept a less desirable state as the one that will be created.

Your mind-body connection is strong and works in constant communication, each doing its best to support the highest functioning of your physical self until something is out of physical alignment. In these moments, the mind begins to panic, and choices are made. Those choices are generally not made consciously. The mind works quickly to get the conditions under control, so fast that you may not even know what happened. The result is that you have begun a cycle of choices and decisions that take you further and further away from your ideal state. In this disconnect, we find ourselves unclear about how we arrived at this new state and unsure of what to do. Again, you may find yourself in a moment where you want to take a deep breath. You can choose to be enticed or even excited at this moment. This is where you begin to unlock the power within yourself.

There is one immediate difference as we shift from the mind-body connection to the spiritual self. The spiritual self sees you as whole and needing no protection from yourself. It recognizes that when in alignment, nothing else is required. In some faiths, this is the place of peace where man and God are one. In others, it is the place where the Holy Spirit is in control within the vessel.

In the spiritual self, you are whole and capable of everything, including self-healing. The spiritual self is rooted in faith. The strength of actualized faith may differ, but everyone has the capacity to operate in full faith. Many have performed Miracles, Signs, and Wonders in alignment with the strength of their faith. This is powered by faith and the presence of God.

All of this works together to help you process healing. Let's lay it out simply. You are whole and complete with all systems working in alignment. Over time, you learn different things that impact your ability to distinguish between real and perceived risk. When you begin to identify the automatic assumptions that your mind makes relative to the conditions that you are experiencing, the pattern can be interrupted.

Presence and intention help you recognize your true state. By ensuring that both systems work together, one can maximize the benefit of the spiritual self leading the physical self. When the spiritual self leads, the physical self can focus on what is happening in the body and address the ailment from a place of peace and centeredness. The frantic action of protection and danger is quieted as the spiritual self begins to conduct the symphony within the body that is the natural makeup of the self.

Chapter Pearls

- There is always a choice available to you. Recognizing the availability of choices is a part of your healing work.

- All healing comes from God. From that perspective, we can accept our role in healing and honor God as the CEO.

- The Spiritual Self-perspective reminds you that you are already whole and need no protection from yourself. It is safe to begin reframing how you have been exploring the world.

Journal Prompts

- You are worthy and brave. Is anything standing in the way of you fully believing that to be true?

- What is one ah-ha moment you captured during this chapter? What learnings did you derive as a result, and how will you apply them?

Chapter Two

Understanding the Matrix

As human beings, we live in a complex world. People aptly refer to it as the matrix world, which it is. If we were to simplify it, it is a world full of man-created jails. The jails are self-designed and have an open door. Conditioning inside and in the external environment is designed to keep you in a place of limited thinking and to restrict the fullness of your experiences. Imagine that you are in a cell with the door open, but you cannot see that you are even in the cell. Without the perspective of walls or bars, you cannot see the door. You would not look for a door because the reference point for there being a door is seeing the walls and being able to identify that you are in a room. It is complex to understand because we have not allowed the activities that create questions within us, which build our perspective.

You may want to journal to capture your initial emotions attached to this revelation. It is difficult to accept this as truth. That makes sense to you because you never had a reason to contemplate it before, at least not in your conscious mind. Perhaps some of you have given your personal awareness journey, but you might not have had the words to articulate it. Try to explain it to those around you. This time, you will have these words to help you form your own understanding. Yes. This is the truth. Truth is required. The truth is what allows the walls to come into view. Truth helps you accept that you have been in this cell since birth. In your youth, you moved back and forth between the cell and freedom. You remembered more of who you are and your purpose than you do in your current state. This statement would only not be true if babies could read. Beyond infancy, we begin to move less freely between the cell and freedom.

Just A Moment

Take five deep cleansing breaths. Give yourself a moment to center yourself. Breathing deeply to increase the oxygen flow will help you to receive the truth in this section. Remember to breathe whenever you feel stressed or anxious as you ingest these revelations. It often helps to imagine your inhalation bringing you peace and calm while your exhalation releases tension and anxiety. Drinking water is also calming and would benefit your body in this state. Most people are dehydrated, which is a conduit for dis-ease and makes it difficult for things like truth to flow. These are foundations for life, although you may consider them 'self-care.' There are reasons that you do not regularly monitor these things, and they are connected to the matrix. Let's explore.

The expansive mind begins to unravel the constructs of this world. It starts to question and eventually challenge the things that have been stated as truths, which encourages you to remain in the cells. In your cell, you will inevitably run into the walls over and over again. You can physically feel the restrictiveness of your prison without having conscious knowledge that is where you are.

Take a moment and observe your surroundings. Whether you're in your room, on the subway, train, or plane, or even just in your backyard or bathroom, these places are familiar to you. You have come to expect certain things to be there. As long as things look and feel familiar, you settle the limbic system discussed in the last chapter. The feeling of being settled, or settling, allows you to accept your current conditions. The mind begins to think; at least I know where I am. This place is what I accept. This is what I should expect.' Read those statements again. They are limited in their current form. It is jarring.

This is the way you think automatically because of the way conditioning occurs. It takes a conscious effort to see your room or your yard differently. As long as you see familiar things, you move toward acceptance. Now, consider that you have been living in your cell since birth. It is actually the most familiar place you know. It stands to reason that being aware of it would be difficult because you have been accepting this place for as long as you can remember.

At some point, going back and forth between the cell and beyond became taxing. Every time you left your cell, you met new conditions and unexpected challenges because things were new. You heard discouraging things about yourself, your choices, and your lack of knowledge. Over time, the rhetoric spewed at one another, especially to children, breaks our spirit.

You stop looking for freedom. You decide that being comfortable is less painful. In this place, you manage expectations and minimize the value you bring to the world. This is when the cell begins to gain the upper hand. The world begins to declare its victory over your spirit.

The good news is that you have had moments where you have pushed yourself past the limitations of comfort. You chose to move somewhere new, or perhaps you took a new job, finished college, or learned to play an instrument. These experiences begin to create the euphoric feeling that helps propel you forward.

There is a limit to what you can truly feel in the cell, so you begin to want more and more experiences that push you beyond your comfort zone. This is when you begin to long for more. Longing is not enough to help you recognize your surroundings, but it is part of what propels you to keep looking. When you elevate your awareness, you simultaneously begin to see the cracks in the foundation. Light begins appearing in places where it wasn't before, sparking your curiosity.

So now, you are clamoring to get out. Yes, and you should. Congratulations on accepting another truth. Journal about the hope and freedom you are sensing in this moment. This is good news. What is even more exciting is that you are your own key. Yes, you are the key. You can leave your cell anytime you want! You even remember where the door is; you are beginning to sense it again as you did when you were younger. You are understandably eager to get out, but do not skip ahead. The door is, was, and always will be open. It's simply a decision for you. There is more to understand about why you have remained in this place for so long. As we move through this section, *you will gain the understanding you need to process why you have been there and assess your readiness to leave.*

Before you decide to loathe the cell, remember this: it kept you safe, even if it was restrictive by its very nature. It was a home for you that created a sense of comfort to soothe you during difficult times. Once you depart from it, you will find that staying "grounded" becomes more difficult. The process of staying grounded will require focus and practice. It may be beneficial for you to have support during this part of the journey. There are coaches, programs, and energy workers who can explain and support grounding more robustly during your transition.

Simply put, you will experience freedom when you move from your constant habitation in your cell. Freedom is exhilarating because it lacks the restrictive nature you experienced in your cell. It is also without all the grounding principles, facts, stories, and experiences you have had that helped you understand your life in the cell.

Imagine that you said yes to going on a journey when you woke up this morning. You didn't stop to consider what to bring, the weather, activities, or the environment. Upon leaving, you begin to feel unprepared because you simply do not have the information you typically gather before you take a trip. For most, the imagination immediately conjures up a beautiful place, representing the elements you love most — perhaps a historic city, a mountainous region, a rainforest, a lake, or a beach. You have now begun to create expectations of how you will feel and what you will do when you arrive. Instead of the place you imagined, you arrive at a place with just earth beneath your feet. There is no grass. There are no trees, houses, cars, or even the typical sounds you hear daily. There are no other people. It is as if you are standing in the center of a blank canvas, with the artist staring intently at it, deciding what to create. This is not what you are accustomed to experiencing. This is what the experience will feel like over and over again as you begin to leave the cell.

You will experience being the painter, and rather than calling it 'creation,' think about it in terms of revealing your existence to yourself in a new way. Once you convince your wired body and mind that this is a safe and real place, you will begin to experience the freedom you have. That freedom will allow you to create your experience. Creation requires that you loosen your grip on what is. It will require that you loosen your ties to what you have believed to be true and what you have been taught in your traditional upbringing. As your grip releases, the euphoria of this new place begins to sweep you away. Without some grounding, you will feel untethered. This process is most effective when it is gradual and when you have support.

Why would you want to leave your cell? If the experiences are new, push you beyond your comfort zone, and require you to stay grounded, is it worth it? You can choose your freedom at any time. It requires your choice. You can choose to go back or make choices that immediately bring you back to your cell. The choice is and always will be yours. The answer you seek is simple. Truth exists outside of your cell.

This is why perspective is so important. Inside your cell are limitations to what you can do, what you want, and how you choose to live and engage in the world. As you might imagine, the cell only allows you to grow to a certain point. Imagine a giant inside a small treasure box. If every time they try to stand, their head crashes into the ceiling, it stands to reason that they will eventually stop trying to stand. Numerous studies support the notion that our surroundings, including the environment, influence behavior. If your current environment will only support growth to a certain level, you find yourself at a point of decision. Will you choose to stop growing, or will you choose a new environment? The answer may seem simple, but the fact that your cell is unseen adds a layer of complexity.

Take, for example, a single parent with four children, two girls and two boys. They live in a small home with two bedrooms. The children sleep in the two bedrooms, and the parent has converted the small living room into their bedroom. Their only space for recreation and gathering is their kitchen. To create comfort for the children, the parent makes a sacrifice. Every night, when the parent goes to bed, they dream about a house with more bedrooms. One additional bedroom would make a world of difference in how they rest, engage with one another, and experience comfort. The parent constantly thinks of ways to earn more and save to buy a larger home. The tension created within their experience acts as a catalyst for change.

Even though a compelling reason is present and evident every day, some people will not make the choice to move. The factors that lead to the decision to remain in a state of suffering are varied. Even in this example, we can say they have a good life. They are safe, there is a place to sleep, and the parent is willing to sacrifice to care for others. It is worth noting that for many, we would not consider the conditions described in their home as suffering. For many, the dream of simply owning a home feels beyond their reach. Some families have three or more generations living in the same home, which can be an apartment or a house. That can be a truly beautiful experience. They would not view this as suffering at all and would likely thrive with any change in condition.

Your reaction to the example is worth noting. This is a clue that will help you assess the conditions of others with your own experience. Take some time to journal about your response here. What was your initial reaction? How did you feel as you imagined their experience? Did you compare it to your own experience? What did you find there?

This example is important for several reasons. First, suffering is not equal; what one person considers suffering may differ from another. ***We often fail to appreciate the struggles of others when their experiences don't directly relate to our own,*** especially when we are immersed in the matrix world. We are unwilling to consider that others' suffering may be more painful than our own. Humans are wired to believe that their circumstances are the most difficult to navigate until they begin to truly develop empathy.

One of the most compelling reasons to leave the cell is to begin seeing yourself in relation to others in a genuine way. This is a place where people learn to see one another without judgement or assuming how the conditions came to be. You've not asked yourself how your conditions came to be. You accepted that there were situations you experienced and that you have been living in a cell you cannot see. That is not quite enough. The next question is, "How did I get here? What choices did I make? How aware was I of those choices?" Now, consider for a moment that those very same questions are ones that you may find yourself using when you look at the lives of others.

From the comfortable perch inside our cell, we look out at the lives of others, unaware that we, too, share similar conditions. It is simply easier to see someone else's choices and conditions than the pain we experience when we look at our own. Leaving the cell requires your willingness to look at your own choices and conditions. You can refer to them as your shadows; the things that are always there but that we avoid viewing or contemplating.

We can return our attention there if you acknowledge that you asked about leaving the cell. You want to leave because you are beginning to recognize that there is more. Even your ego is on board now. It is saying, "I can do what they do. I don't want to be left behind." It is ok. Everyone's ego is selfish and self-centered. You can control it, but at this moment, bring your awareness to the pull of wanting to know, do, and be more.

This is why. It is this feeling. This desire to know more, to experience the fullness of life. To allow yourself to expand. Remember the giant in the treasure box? The giant was just reminded of their strength and might. They decide to stand up and toss the lid off the box. Imagine the giant standing there, one half of its body in the box and the other exposed to the fullness of the world around it. Now they have a choice.

Stay here in comfort, or step out onto the blank canvas and begin to explore and create. This is that choice point, and you are right there with the giant. Journal about what you are choosing and WHY. It is your personal WHY that will keep you moving forward when it is difficult. Your WHY reminds you that it is worth it, that you are worth it. This is one of the most important moments for you to contemplate and journal. Take your time. The book will be here when you're ready to delve deeper.

There is a pull to keep you in your cell, and it is quite powerful. More than anything, it uses the desire to stay in a place of comfort to keep you contemplating staying put. It is incredibly powerful. Your desire for comfort often prevails, keeping you small and contained.

In contrast, think of when you were a child. You desired to be free. Whether you played outside or allowed yourself to be transported in books, you found ways to be free. This sense of freedom was a driving factor in your life. Once you learned to crawl, you began to experience the freedom that comes with it. It helped you to explore and to become fascinated with the world. You were not afraid of what you might find. You were not afraid to explore; in fact, you were certain that exploration was your reason for living. You found yourself thirsting for knowledge and satisfying it through your favorite senses. This was how you allowed yourself to operate in childhood and perhaps in your early adulthood.

The environment began to constrict you as you became more knowledgeable. Between your own experiences and what you were taught, you began to fear the unknown. For some, the impact made them avoid people, places, and situations that were new and different. This is where the isms are born- sexism, racism, classism, and where the superiority of religion becomes the way we sort people and then experience.

Once the paradigms changed and the fearfulness of the unknown became a core part of your frame of reference, you began to shift away from what was new and different. Some might argue that, like the limbic system, some of this autonomic response serves a protective function.

This is true in a sense, but it is an overactive response, often creating fear where it is not even warranted. It holds a person back from experiences that broaden their perspective and help to expand their minds. As you allowed yourself to be influenced by the way fear began to affect you, your willingness to try new things shifted. Rather than longing for new experiences, gaining security became the main focus. For many, the quest for a life that minimized pain, change, and conflict became more important than the actual experience of life or quality of life. This is the foundation for what you refer to as a 'mid-life crisis. As you begin to remember who you are and feel the inevitable pull against comfort and the desire to experience life in alignment, you become torn between the emotions of two ideals.

What you call a 'mid-life crisis can actually happen at any time. When the recognition of being out of alignment is allowed to permeate your awareness, it creates the conditions for internal unrest. This is what you call a crisis. The truth is that the crisis started when you stopped experiencing the newness of life. It is likely that you didn't realize that the limitations around you had become your jailer. It is because you did not have the awareness of what true alignment feels like that you did not know that there was even an issue. Basically, you could not really experience it without contrasting what was possible. Think about the concept of "knowing." Once you have the inkling that there is something else to be considered or to contrast, your mind begins to test and explore. The feeling of "knowing" creates new connections that challenge what you currently hold as the experience you are having. You can liken it to looking through a zoomed-in lens that appears to be looking down on a mouse in a small box. Imagine the lens begins to retract, and eventually, you can see that there is a mouse in the center of a large maze. Both were true at the same time; the box and the maze existed. Looking through the zoomed-in lens gave you the impression that there could only be one reality. That mirrors the experience you had before new information was provided.

Having a clear perspective on the current experience contributes to the feeling of safety. Once we are unclear about existing conditions, insecurity begins to creep in. When you are open to possibilities, you typically hold the notion that the current situation is what you know it to be, but there is space in your mind for it to be more. That significantly affects whether or not you begin to feel insecure. The feeling of security lessens when you know that there is a genuine state of being in alignment. It is safe to admit that the comfort you experienced before you knew alignment was possible made you feel grounded and secure, as defined by the world.

Pause for a moment to reflect. What does it feel like to experience security? How secure do you really feel? It is remarkable that one can even create a sense of security based on external factors. The current climate is very unstable. Consider the transient nature of things around you. Some considerations include your job/company, your home, societal unrest, pandemics, hunger, homelessness, and mental exhaustion. The swirl created by the inconsistency of conditions outside of you threatens to pull you in at any moment. Take another look. Is what you have considered security, in fact, is it secure? No. In this experience, the pieces outside you are not secure.

Things do not satisfy the need for security. You've watched millionaires end up destitute. You have seen people pilfer their riches. You have watched people make decisions that created risk, only to have everything they had taken away. Considering the market's volatility, intentional scamming that casts a negative light on bitcoin, as well as some of the devastating financial scandals and schemes, it is clear that the financial reality of our world does not offer true security. We look for circumstances to build a wall of safety. Consider the person who spent multiple decades at a single employer, only to find themselves jobless due to a layoff. The things and circumstances that use or offer the image of security are falling away, and it is undeniably time to seek truth.

As a result of the eroding image of safety, people are experiencing a disconnect. It is an untethering of sorts. The increasing uncertainty begins to make people edgy and distrustful. Their behavior begins to match the discontent within. As a result, people are beginning to implode. They are so fearful and angry that they are unsure of how to continue. Many are even driven by the desire to exact vengeance on others simply because of the unrest within that results from things they may not recognize in themselves. When there is unresolved trauma and fear-based behavior, unhealed conditions exist. No, these things do not create security. Believing in them is a catalyst for creating more fear. The constant generation of fear is what creates a crisis. The crisis then becomes your emotional captor, and the cycle continues from there.

If you have experienced or watched someone trying to lose weight, you have likely seen the phenomenon of weight loss plateau. They are doing all the same things, but results have slowed, and they are not seeing the same pace of progress. The lack of progress creates doubt. They are no longer assured that they can continue to lose weight at the same pace. Many will unconsciously decide that they don't believe that there is value in continuing. They begin to create a reality of comfort around settling into the plateau. They will stay there, creating a narrative that allows them to feel comfortable where they are. The narrative becomes their truth. The original intent has been replaced, and they have rewired themselves to believe this milestone in their weight loss journey is enough. The constant re-contracting within creates the conditions for stagnation. It happens so easily that the person does not even realize they have just given up on their own plan. The desire to avoid the emotional pain of disappointment permeates their decision-making. The cycle continues with the individual realizing that what was a desire to accept comfort was actually settling. Settling was an act of trading out their desire for their defined outcome for comfort. That is at the core of conditioning in your lives. That conditioning pulls you out of alignment over and over again. This is the impact of being within the matrix.

If we look more closely at our friend on the weight loss journey, we see that as they realize they have settled, they begin to look for proof that their choice to accept where they are is ok. Proof comes from others who have paused their weight loss progress. Looking for people they used to see in the gym who no longer show up to work out may speak to almost being okay with achieving a goal and changing behavior. A reduction in clothing size may make them feel satisfied with some progress, forgetting that the goal may have been to drop two sizes. They look for justifications that help them cement the decision in their minds. More time is spent on rationalizing their choice than evaluating how much time and effort it would take to actually reach their initial goal. When the initial goal was established, there was no middle ground. The goal-setting process did not include an early release clause. Although milestones may have been established, they do not necessarily equate to the finish line in the contest.

Now for the difficult part. You have been this person. You have been and possibly are at this very moment. It is an uncomfortable truth that can be countered by the mere fact that you are reading this book. Take a deep breath. All is well. You need to recognize these aspects of yourself to generate the desire to change. **On the next leg of this journey, you will need to learn how to create comfort in places that are milestones, not your finish line.** You need to see the patterns and signals of things that help your mind move from accomplishment to settling. Settling is not your destination.

Where have you seen yourself trade your goals for comfort? Perhaps you have stopped on the path to achievement because someone around you became uncomfortable with your growth. What rooms are you in that encourage you to silence your voice? These are some of the ways that you have become comfortable in the matrix. This is what the matrix seeks to do: to remind you of the comfort of playing small. It reminds you that change can create discomfort for you and those you love. It encourages you to believe that you can only receive love if you allow your desires to be managed by your effort to appease others. Your benchmark for achievement becomes a standard benchmark, shared by all and controlled by the environment in the matrix.

Many of the concepts we see in psychology and sociology provide additional emphasis on the impact of the matrix. Group behavior shows us that human nature is predisposed to conform. Group dynamics become a prevalent way of being as we go through adolescence and become emphasized as we enter adulthood. There are social experiments that support the knowledge of conforming behavior. At the same time, the individuals desire rebellion and individuality, but the pull of group dynamics is powerful.

Take the example of the elevator study (referenced from Bethany Lutheran Univ). A camera was placed in the elevator to observe group behavior. Actors were staged in the elevator facing the back wall. Each time the elevator doors opened, people walked in with a perplexed look on their faces. The newcomer almost always turned around to face the back wall. For those who didn't, they struggled with the decision. Even though many had likely ridden elevators before, they were tempted or did not follow the group's actions. Even though their conviction to stay facing forward was there, it wasn't strong enough to keep many from turning around.

It is interesting to observe. It is also interesting that a norm says you should face forward in the elevator in the first place. The different behavior is noticeable because it is commonplace to face forward. That illuminates two points for us. First, we can ignore what feels right and normal when the alternative is connected to our desire to be a part of the whole.

Secondly, people have become so used to norms (and following them) that deviating feels entirely wrong. We cannot see ourselves deviating, even when we don't see why it matters. Looking towards the elevator door makes practical sense. You can see the change in floors, prepare to exit the lift, and observe people stepping in and out, which provides a sense of security. You could also achieve the same experience by stepping in and turning sideways. Peripheral vision is efficient as well. We don't even allow ourselves the opportunity to explore what might make sense because we have been conditioned to do what we see others do.

This makes it inherently difficult to break away from matrix thinking. We desire to be a part of the whole, so we spend a good majority of our lives learning to blend. As long as things are aligned with most of our values, we can continue to move with the herd. Once the misalignment is obvious, we can no longer continue on that path. We begin to experience misalignment in every sense - we can feel it, see it, hear it, and so on. The questioning of everything becomes a part of our way of being. We cannot unsee that there is dissonance in our experience.

This dissonance is a gift. It is an important clue in our quest to live life in accordance with our purpose. This can be a difficult concept to face. No one desires to have the truth exposed to them, which can be potentially painful. However, we must have these experiences to serve as catalysts as we continue on our journey.

In essence, the matrix is a co-created, ever-evolving fixture that helps us define life in its simplest terms. It removes the expansiveness that is truth. The simplification feeds our egos and generates the perception of power. The truth is that if people truly understood the vastness of what is possible within them and then allowed themselves to tap into the Divine's expansiveness, they would be unstoppable.

We have explored what makes the matrix so important. It does a great job of reinforcing what you have decided is important. The matrix environment reminds you that you are successful when you do the things that everyone else is doing the same way. Those operating outside of the matrix are labeled extremists or unstable unless they present their information in a way that makes them seem relatable. Often, relatability is a form of admiration. They may be very wealthy, provide specialized knowledge, or even simply be of a race or nationality that the masses accept. The matrix reinforces the ideals generated by the masses and joins those concepts with the cyclical nature of the hamster wheel. Secret societies would not have to exist if the world did not operate with different types of "rules and regulations" depending on who you are, where your family is from, the wealth amassed by your family, and whether or not you have decided to allow the matrixed environment to hold you within its paradigm.

With a greater understanding of what the matrix is and how it specializes in conformity, we can begin to operate differently. Some people will understand this dynamic and be appalled by the type of control and influence that has been exerted over them. Many others will be confused, and some will even experience disbelief. Each reaction is ok. Your reaction will be directly related to your readiness to understand and accept the truth. There is no judgement here. The reality is that much of this will be a relief for those who have been seeking truth. It confirms what you have known. You may have had pieces and can now string them together to make sense of it all. For others, you may have to come back to this section a few times after having heard the truth so that you can engage in your own experimentation as you operate in the world. The critical thing to recognize is that you need the exact level of truth and matrix thinking to arrive at the point you are at today. You required it. It kept you safe. It helped you make sense of the world. You made choices you believed were the best at each moment until now. It's less about right and wrong choices; rather, it is about the action of assessing what you know to be true and deciding based on those conditions.

Spend no time opining on what you should have done. There is no such thing. For every choice, a door opens, and there are more choices. There are many paths, and all are ok. Lessons will come, and you will navigate them. Some lessons you may repeat. Some you may avoid altogether. The path is what it is. While there is an optimal path, all paths are ok. You get both what you need and are ready to receive.

What matters is now, the current moment. This truth. How will you allow the truth you are ingesting to begin to open you up to possibilities? Will you allow yourself to consider your true potential? How will you decide to operate around the matrix? What will you begin to question? These are the best prompts for your meditation time in the upcoming days. This is a great time to take a break and journal for a while. Do your best to avoid the judgement of self and others.

Everyone is doing what they believe to be their best, even when it looks like they should "know better." The word "should" is a powerful matrix tool. Should implies that something is not good enough where it is. It encourages you to question choices and to second-guess yourself. When you commence second-guessing, the reference point you use is... that's right, the matrix. "What are other people doing? Am I too different? If I do this, will I be out of sync with others?" Learn to replace should with something definitive. "I will" or "I won't" are great places to start. Make a decision and finalize the process. Precious time is wasted on "should," and it keeps you locked in the current moment with limited thinking.

Please take some deep breaths and spend some time journaling. You are right where you need to be. If you accept the truth that is present at this moment, you can choose to grow.

Chapter Pearls

- The matrix is a simple description of our self-designed jail. The door is always open, and your journey of self-discovery helps you see it.

- Awareness and choice are your keys to freedom from the matrix.

- You should be equally grateful for the lessons you learn within the matrix and for those you learn outside of it. Each offers perspective and learning relevant to your life's journey.

Journal Prompts

- How will you allow the truth you are ingesting to begin to open you up to possibilities?

- What will you begin to question about the matrix? What do you most want to explore?

Chapter Three

The Power of the Collective

We have explored the backdrop of perspective- our early mindsets, experiences, and the matrix. It's time to explore the role each of us plays within the collective. We are the collective. The human race. We will use the term collective interchangeably with 'humanity' and the 'human race.' All of us are a part of the collective by design, even though some people may not identify in that way. One way to understand the collective is to imagine a gathering of all people surrounded by peace. Each is whole unto itself, yet part of the gathering. In this chapter, we will explore people's relationship with the collective and the power available when we recognize that our connection is by divine design.

Some people will choose to disassociate themselves from the collective, typically desiring to elevate themselves by absolving themselves from feeling responsible for anyone else. That responsibility can stem from being accountable for shared experiences to acknowledging that they have created conditions that limit the ascension of others. Many more have yet to awaken to their true role as a part of the collective.

The collective is not seen in the way humans typically categorize themselves —race, gender, socio-economic status, education, working class, etc. The collective is simply a term for everyone. The fantastic aspect is that everything is connected. Each person influences and/or impacts the others. This is actually a blessing when you choose to embrace our true selves and purpose.

Examples of smaller subgroups in society help us understand the power that exists when people choose to honor their role as a part of the collective. There are many "brotherhood and sisterhood" organizations in the world: civic groups, clubs, scouts, sororities and fraternities, unions, police, masons, and intensely secretive societies where much of the direction and influence for the world is determined.

Take a major corporation as an example. Of the tens of thousands of employees who work in a company, significant decisions are generally made by a small leadership group of fewer than ten people. Those ten are believed to know the function they represent, have expertise in the industry, a firm commitment to the future of the business, and the best interests of the people served. Boards of directors work similarly, aligning with the strategic direction of the business and making decisions about the organization's future. Typically, multiple methods are employed to ensure that there is feedback and appropriate context, allowing the group to have the relevant information needed to make informed decisions. The mechanisms often include shareholder interests, briefings from the leadership, and data, including the voice of the customer, as well as the culture or employees' pulse checks. The board is small in number but has the decision-making power to reject a business's strategic plan. They have the authority to influence the direction of the business through their decisions.

When small groups make decisions for the larger group without mechanisms to gather feedback from those impacted, it sets the stage for failure. These small groups tend to converse only amongst themselves, often sharing similar experiences, which increases the likelihood of making decisions that benefit them rather than the entire group. While representing the whole is not impossible, it requires shedding self-interest, fear, and a scarcity mindset.

Understanding scarcity as a mindset is crucial. If you are unfamiliar with the term, you may have formed the opinion that this mindset is held by those in lower socio-economic standing than those "representing" them. It may surprise you to know that this mentality is a driving force for many in power. Even those with decision-making roles may operate from a scarcity mindset. This creates the conditions for fear-based decision-making. The notion that "sharing means we won't have enough" implies that those with more resources would temporarily need to accept having less than they prefer in order to invest in and support the individuals they are responsible for representing. The belief that there is no endless and everlasting supply of all necessary resources to meet our needs is fundamentally flawed. If we operated with an abundance mindset and designed systems to thrive as a collective, we could tap into more than we would ever need. The current constructs keep us from seeing the truth. If people were puzzle pieces needed to complete the board, we would actively ensure that each piece got into place. If completion meant we accessed full abundance for today and forever, we would waste no time completing the puzzle. Scarcity has led many to believe that we are not yet in the midst of experiencing the real-life implications of the great puzzle. In truth, we are in precisely that place. The puzzle will remain incomplete if we continue to allow scarcity to rule.

We may not be able to visibly see the path to all that we need, but that is why innovation is powerful. Historically, when faced with challenges and no obvious way to handle a situation, you spring into action to figure out or "make a way." This kind of "possibilities" thinking or growth mindset is divine. It aligns with faith and the belief that there is always a provision. Provision comes from the divine. People who operate in scarcity create an excuse to hoard what they have from others rather than challenge themselves to think about what else is possible. With the expansive nature of Spirit, we should know that there is always a way.

Let's examine an example from the Bible and Christianity. Jesus fed the masses, 5000 people, with two fish and five loaves of bread. The disciples saw that the hour was late and understood that the people were hungry. Jesus' instruction was to "give them something to eat." Rather than worrying about whether it would be enough, Jesus trusted that God had provided. Jesus looked up to God with thankfulness, broke the bread, and gave it to the disciples to distribute. The Bible says, "They all ate and were satisfied." It should be noted that there was also some left over. (Matthew 14:13-21 NIV) In your finite mind, the question is likely, "How could that little feed so many?" For a moment, ask a different question. "Why do we start out believing it will not be enough?"

Our experience and perspective influence how we think. We may not believe that two fish and five loaves could ever be enough, but it's not really about the amount of food. It is about the feeling of being satiated. Take it a step further. People have fasted for days, weeks, even, without food. When the fasts are spiritual, people speak of being satiated even though they haven't eaten. Couldn't a person feel full from the lesson and experience of being in the presence of the Divine, God, and be just grateful for whatever morsels they received?

Another lesson we can derive is the importance of community. Assume for a moment that as each person considered that they were one of 5000, they recognized that the needs of others might be greater than their own. I imagine none wanted to be so gluttonous that they would take so much that others might have nothing. Their being in proximity to one another created a sense of community and accountability. "If I take too much, you might not have anything at all. I choose to take a reasonably small amount- enough to satiate me and ensure you also have what you need." There was not a person eating half of a fish and a whole loaf of bread in that large crowd. Why? The presence of God was there. They were in an environment where they recognized themselves as part of the collective. They thought more broadly than themselves. This gives significant insight into people's behavior.

Society today is structured in a way that allows those who have a lot to separate themselves from those who have very little. The system makes it easy for people to choose to avoid seeing what they have in common with others. Instead of focusing on generating more, people focus on taking as much of what is present as they can.

The mindset of looking more broadly at how to generate more and to teach others to generate while sharing wealth is biblical. There is no value to hoarding while society is deteriorating. It will inevitably lead to your demise because society is in turmoil. Whether through economic collapse or an uprising of those who have been oppressed, eventually, the shift will occur. If you allow yourself to be blinded by your current situation and ignore what is happening in the balance of your collective, you will fall. We are connected, and there is more than enough present and more that can be generated when we are willing to understand our responsibility extends beyond ourselves and our immediate family.

Social media has created ways for people to pop in and out of society, creating what feels like a presence while intentionally separating themselves from society. This "false presence" is actually what fuels the divide between people. It creates a false narrative that clouds the collective. While social media is an integral part of our culture today, it does not foster genuine connectivity between people. In real life, you can't swipe away from seeing everything you don't wish to see.

People fear what would happen if they were to trade places with people who are different from them. Their propensity is to complain about where they are and to be unwilling to give it up at the same time. They reject their current circumstances while acknowledging internally that they don't have it "that bad." In the next moment, they look at people around them with pity or sometimes even distaste for the circumstances and conditions of others. They quickly make assumptions about how they got there, never considering the choices they made that keep them in their current circumstances.

The notion of not being willing to consider trading places with others is essential. Even though the changing of places is theoretical, people resist even imagining it. This indicates that there is an internal recognition of the differences people experience. All situations are not the same. People are not treated equally. The just societies desire a more consistent foundational experience for all people. Differences emerge through their choices and efforts, not through systematic oppression. When you consider the notion of what it is like to be in any community that is treated as less than the majority, you allow yourself to acknowledge the truth. The truth is that not everyone has a consistent experience. People do not have the exact same foundation.

As generations progress, the gaps have gotten wider and wider. People use the experiences of a few who have managed to break through circumstances as if to say it is possible for everyone. That is not true, and you know that in your heart. We reject the notion because accepting it means that we have to change. This is one of the greatest struggles we have as humanity. We will never reach our full potential individually when there is so much struggle within the collective.

People who have amassed a significant amount of wealth engage in philanthropy because they know that the imbalance is impacting their soul's experience. The urge to do "something" stems from the mind seeking a way to absolve itself of the responsibility to support change. The individual suffers when the collective suffers. Those who seem to have amassed a large amount of wealth and have the appearance of everything going their way will suffer as well. There must be reconciliation between one another. Societal systems will require more than reform. They require a redesign

A true representation of all people needs to be present. The shift will require taking appropriate measures to reconcile the differences in experiences levied on people. It will differ by continent, country, state, and even county. No single blueprint will be able to create a universal shift, but appropriate focus, mindset, and heart for truth will usher forth the new way. The universal shift will unfold as the healing work progresses. That work must be ongoing in the individual and the collective.

There will be more discussion about what to do to heal, but for now, focus on who. Collectively, people are required to create change, which will occur through healing. That change starts with a pure heart and the right spirit. It requires a commitment to introspection and change within. Healing is being open to change and seeking ways to evolve from your current patterns. You must begin to love yourself truly in order to have love for humanity. With love as the central and universal binding force, anything is possible. Without that, progress will be temporary and regressive.

The collective's intentions are incredibly powerful. Gatherings of people committed to making a measurable difference in the world can and will change the world. The collective power can be leveraged for good or for the demise of humanity. The way that we engage people to mobilize matters. In today's society, fear is used to influence behavior above anything else. It has become even rarer for people to fight back against fearfulness. When fear is avoided, it creates the space for generating even more fear.

In the same way, an individual can decide to use fear as fuel; the collective can dissipate fear. As the collective rises into power, any stance it takes to minimize or eliminate fear will propel the whole forward. As the collective naturally evolves its mindset to common goals and outcomes, navigation through fear becomes the norm. As the collective stands boldly in the face of fear, the individuals strengthen their resolve, independent of the whole. The aligned movement of the collective has a significant role in elevating the individual. There is more to explore here in a later chapter, building on the premise of the central soul.

The Black Experience

One of the best examples of the need to reconcile the differentiation of experiences can be seen in the U.S. Black/African American people have a significantly different experience from that of any other race or ethnic group in the country. Case studies after case studies should be conducted on the experiences of African Americans in America. Indeed, people of color, especially black people, have been the recipients of much harm and trauma in the U.S. as acculturation has occurred. Their treatment has been deplorable and in no way mirrors the Divine's intention for them. There are so many case studies that can be generated about how people overcome systematic oppression, the impact of redlining, and food control, access, and simply the effect of continued hatred and disrespect on an entire group of people.

Despite the horrors of the black experience, both historically and what is transpiring in the modern day, their contributions to society continue to be immense. Innovation, Music and entertainment, food, social design, and trends are all areas where the impact of Black people can be experienced. The arts are influenced by authors, screenwriters, songwriters, and singers, as well as some of the best movies and shows. As a people who have been intentionally dis-empowered, they continue to persevere. No other culture is more consistently depicted as useless, hopeless, and poor than that of blacks.

Culturally, it appears that blacks have less readily identifiable cultural norms and practices than what you see across other groups of people of color. This is by design. There are incredible cultural norms that exist. However, the images and portrayal of blacks erode their culture. The suppression of the truth about their heritage, contributions, and the impending erasure of their whole history is designed to further distance them from one another. The intent to bring blacks into white America to assimilate was a brilliant design to keep blacks from seeing who they truly are. No other group has faced a consistent expectation of denouncing their heritage to gain acceptance from the majority. There are cultural norms that suggest certain cultures or racial groups excel in specific areas. Blacks are typically told that they can excel in things that whites continue to have ultimate authority and power over. Fields like music, entertainment, and athletics are solid examples. Their collective contributions as a race have entirely changed the dynamic of these arenas, yet they have the smallest portion of ownership.

It is clear that the contributions of Black Americans do not reflect the reality of their lived experiences in this country. While many groups have faced marginalization, the treatment of Black individuals remains deeply entrenched and widely recognized. Activist and educator Jane Elliott underscored this truth in one of her lectures when she asked a group of white participants if they would be willing to trade places with a Black person in America. Not a single person raised their hand. She then pointed out the obvious: if they weren't willing to accept that experience for themselves, they must already know it is unjust (Elliott). The truth is simple: we know it's not right. And while some continue to offer justifications, excuses, or deflections, at the core is a truth we cannot ignore. Every person deserves to be treated with the same dignity and respect we expect for ourselves.

> *"I have always found it curious that people who have experienced oppression can disassociate with it enough to actively engage in the oppression of others. We know it happens, but why aren't we more curious about what fuels that behavior enough to stop it?"-Anika Apple*

The experience of blacks in America is certainly not the only global example of how societal systems need to be reformed.

There are many. A deeper look reveals humanity's pervasive and guttural behaviors: fear and power. When people believe that something that belongs to them is threatened, they will do almost anything to protect themselves. American rhetoric is increasingly casting fear into the hearts of those who are not black to encourage acceptance of the erasure of history and, inevitably, the removal of rights. Who stands to gain as these things occur? This is an example of the collective moving with a fear-based mindset.

To heal, fears must be addressed through truth. For many black Americans, there is an overwhelming sense of exhaustion connected to the need to prove worthiness while fighting to keep what is their birthright. No one should have to fight for what is already theirs. God created all men and women to have equal rights, and is the entity that determines worthiness. There is a requirement for truth and reconciliation to occur in order to create an appropriate redesign for societal culture. Healing will be a required part of setting the groundwork for the shifts that need to occur. In all cases, humanity has the opportunity to begin the process of shifting the narrative and taking massive action for change. It has to begin with truth. One can be absolutely certain that God is on the side of truth and love for all, not simply one race of people. The same can be said for preference of gender. To assume that God is aligned with the mistreatment or intentional destruction of any of Their children, black, homeless, indigent, lower class/caste, or other marginalized people, would be gravely incorrect. God has designed the world with all of its people to live in peace and abundance. Man is responsible for whether or not that is the current existence. Wherever that is not witnessed, it should be a sign that change must come, and Healing Is Required.

Collective Intentions

Intentions are powerful. There is a medical definition for intention that you may not be aware of. It speaks to the plan to address a wound. You likely know intention to be defined as a focus or concerted effort. In this case, both are incredibly powerful. Humanity is incredibly wounded. A visual representation would show a body covered with bruises and open sores. The wounds would overlap, revealing the depth of the flesh. You would have places where you see bone and even the evidence of infection. It is not a pretty picture.

That is the same as what you see when you take an honest look at the world. You have become desensitized to the magnitude of the impact on the "body- the visual representation." You may want to reject that notion, but the clear answer is yes in a space of honesty with a pure heart. We know this because if there were no collective desensitization, the world would look different. This book would be different if it were even necessary. It is the grave state that we are in that should be a call to action, an emotional plea to act in the best interest of humanity. This is a moment of choice. What will you do as the knowledge is presented to you?

It is possible that hearing this truth may impact you. It is understandable. Examining the evidence, we observe that the deterioration of the collective has been ongoing for centuries. You may have a few causes that are incredibly personal and some that you contribute to from afar. There may be others that you have an interest in addressing, but have not identified a way to create an impact. If you consider the activism of those in your family and your closest network, you can likely see the evidence of desensitization. The beauty of this moment is that you are willing to see and accept the truth. As unsettling as it may be, the truth is required if change is to occur.

You cannot identify a problem that you are unwilling to define. You cannot solve a problem that you are unwilling to face. The current way of operating in humanity is to create separation and division. You may call it hierarchy, status, class, belief systems, or even religion. Perhaps it is simply the division of people by gender, race & ethnicity, nationality, and lifestyle. The constant desire to separate oneself from the masses or divide by any criteria erodes humanity.

Shortly after the creation of the world, man was created and then began to procreate. Leaders and citizens of various nations had the same father. The varied "tribes" created identities that, over time, became adversarial in nature. The misalignment of competition and power evolved from the nature of man, not the designs of the Creator.

Over time, many earthly leaders with human voices have sought to unite. Their divine wisdom and ability to see the deterioration of humanity revealed their purpose. As they spoke messages of Love for all, Justice, Equality, and the tenets of compassion and understanding, they faced persecution. Many were jailed, beaten, exiled, and, of course, killed. This provides additional evidence that there is a desire to ignore the problem. As leaders arise and globally observed incidents of egregious behavior occur, there is a consistent long-term response of deafening silence.

There may be immediate concern and intervention from various groups of people, typically focused on a specific area of personal or business interest, followed by an apathetic response. The cycles of inaction and apathy deter many who desire change. Fear immobilizes most of humanity from speaking out and taking action. The desire to fit in and exist quietly, rather than draw attention, has worsened over the last decade. In the current era of social shaming, the tendency to remain quiet is all the more pronounced. There is an uprising in hate, inciting fear and responding in anger. Action often involves writing an inflammatory post or spewing a response without first seeking to understand, both from behind a device. Where are the bridges, those who dare to create connection, in this time of separation? They are mending their wounds and waiting for help. Currently, they are waiting for an army of support from people who are still undecided about whether to get involved.

Take a moment to put yourself in the shoes of each group in this example. Imagine being a part of humanity and being marginalized and treated unjustly while watching the few who have come to support you being mistreated and worse. You would likely begin to lose hope. Transport yourself into being one of the few who rise up against injustice and differentiate yourself to do what you innately know is right. You face persecution from your own family, race, class, etc., and experience persecution for doing what is right, to watch those you desire to help continue to be minimized and underserved. What happens to your fight? Your hope? Your desire to persevere? Consider being part of the group of those who are fearful of speaking out, metaphorically suffocated by the truth of what they see. They fear being excommunicated from their social group. Imagine being choked by their fear. For a moment, put yourself in the place of those who desire continued dissension, driven by greed and power, willing to minimize anyone to ensure that the narrative they perpetuate remains accepted.

Notice the shift in emotion if you can put yourself in their shoes. It's pretty easy to see how it could evolve into anger or even hatred if something threatens to take away the feeling of power. You were able to experience the range of perspectives simply through suggestion and imagination. Consider what it would be like if you were living it-if it were your reality. Do you see why healing must occur? Without each persona's experience with an external truth, they cannot see that their current situation is a result of their wounds. Without a shared belief, moving from your current position is difficult, even if the shift is more desirable. Healing is the process by which an individual begins to recognize their impact on the collective and can more readily choose to make changes.

This is where collective intentionality comes into play. The *Stanford Encyclopedia of Philosophy* defines it as "the power of minds to be jointly directed at objects, matters of fact, states of affairs, goals, or values. Collective intentionality comes in various modes, including shared intention, joint intention, shared belief, collective acceptance, and collective emotion" (Schmid).

When the collective decides to work together to achieve purpose, things can and will change. To motivate the collective to take action, the problem must be pervasive enough to evoke strong emotions and create a risk associated with inaction. For example, when a Caribbean Island experiences the devastation of a hurricane making landfall, the residents come together to rebuild. Neighbors support one another and often provide a safe space for those with uninhabitable dwellings. The varied interests merge together into a collective agenda focused on rebuilding quickly, supporting one another, and protecting economic interests.

The power of the collective can be levied in both thought and action. A compelling vision mobilizes people. A clear call to action and understanding of individual and collective impact create movement. In the current environment, personal interests are at the core of decision-making, and the imposed criteria determine whether to take action. The absence of the collective reasoning for action must be addressed. Individuals often perceive themselves as distinct from the broader human community. In actuality, interconnectedness is what powers humanity. People cannot exist without connection. Life is navigated from a place that focuses on each person in relation to others. The desire to disconnect from the collective is less about the other people and is actually a reflection of how the individual sees themselves.

You may ask how a person can be seen in that way, and it is because they identify with the characteristics and/or behaviors of others that connect with themselves. Those connection points may be favorable or unfavorable. People are attentive to the information that is important to them at any given time. Even seemingly unimportant information may be collected because, internally, there is something that is being interrogated about another person or thing. Let's consider a few examples.

Reflect on the last time you planned to purchase a vehicle. Think about a car make and/or model that you had not considered before, perhaps one that you had never heard of. Simply because it is in your awareness, you notice that vehicle on the road, in parking lots, and even in your neighbor's driveway. You may have passed the vehicle in that driveway once or twice a day for months and never paid attention to it before your search began. It was there as a stimulus, but you did not need it because it was irrelevant to you. The vehicle was not new; you simply had no reason to take it in intentionally because it did not matter.

Consider an acquaintance you have had for several years. Have you ever noticed a habit or behavior that you never noticed before? As you reflect on the experiences that you have had with them, perhaps you recall some other situations where that behavior was present. It may surprise you because it is something that you did not expect to be an issue. For example, a colleague is consistently late to meetings.

In a room of 10 people, perhaps 5 notice it and are annoyed by it. Two may be relieved because it masks their tardiness, and the other three never notice it at all. One day, one of the three who never noticed was presenting to the group. They have 15 minutes to deliver a pitch that typically requires at least 30 minutes, and they need to establish the buy-in of the entire team. They are immediately agitated that the colleague is late and consider it a slight to them because it impacts the presentation window. The team's experiences vary based on their prior experiences. It is reasonable to believe the others who are typically late remain unbothered. The presenter is frustrated and will now be more cognizant of the timeliness of all of their colleagues as well as their own arrival time. The colleagues who are typically annoyed by the late arrival maintain their current countenance. Only the presenter experiences something new because it mattered to them on that day.

Our way of engaging with others is always driven by who we are. That does not mean that it is always self-serving. Our desire to engage may genuinely stem from love and an interest in others. There is value in realizing that, without intentionality, we will capture information that relates mostly to ourselves. If we want to grow in connection to others, we need to do two things consistently. Start by being open to receiving the reflection and asking what you need to do with what you experience. Second, zero in on the person and their experience. You have the capacity to do both when you are intentional about the interaction.

Now that you have allowed the truth to settle in, take some time to journal. What angers you about the state of the collective? What frightens you? How could healing happen? What choices might you make given the additional perspective shared in this chapter?

Chapter Pearls

- The collective, in essence, refers to humanity as a whole, transcending typical societal categorizations such as race, gender, socio-economic status, and education. Each person, consciously or not, impacts and influences the others within this interconnected web.

- Understanding and then choosing to move away from operating with a Scarcity Mindset is critical for the collective's well-being.

- Collective Intentionality is "the power of minds to be jointly directed at objects, matters of fact, states of affairs, goals, or values. When more of the collective decides that healing is required, the momentum needed to shift the world will be present.

- People are attentive to information that has meaning for them at that specific time. This means that other information is present and may be actively missed.

Journal Prompts

- How comfortable were you with putting yourself in the shoes of others? What did you learn about yourself? Are there some actions that came up for you?

- What ideals in this chapter challenged your current ways of thinking the most? What is there for you to explore?

- What ideas do you have about shifting the collective towards healing? What gifts might you bring to that work?

Chapter Four

Tapping into Healing

This is likely the most controversial and challenging statement in the entire book. *You are the only reason you are unhealed.* You. It is the result of your decisions. The wisdom to heal is embedded within the design of your body. The ability to witness your behavior was divinely given to you. Everything you need is accessible, and it always has been. God has made it all possible. The truth is simple. You have always had the answers. They reside within your divine truth, which is a part of your design. You have always had access to the key to your jail- in fact, you are the only true jailer. You have held yourself captive and have been very successful at it.

Healing has always been available to you through the Creator. It is in your seeking and your decision to believe that you deserve healing that the process begins. All too often, circumstances beyond one's control are considered the reason something has not happened. It is time to acknowledge that whether or not you are on your healing journey is a matter of your choice to heal. Yes, it can be difficult to read, and you may find it challenging to accept as you begin to process and journal about it. This is a simple truth that is often overlooked, buried under a complex life filled with circumstances you may or may not have created.

Part of healing is demystifying what has felt complex and elusive. God created you with the ability to heal. All healing comes from God. You've had access to what you need all along, even if you don't fully remember the wisdom They placed within you. Life has a way of layering over the truth, of causing us to forget who we are and what we carry. But healing is required, and remembering is part of the journey..

Take a moment to breathe so that you can begin to unearth the path to your freedom and subsequent healing. Do your best to avoid judgement at this moment. There is only an option to make different choices in the present. The past is already behind you. You deserve grace, so give it to yourself now. That is a part of the healing process.

Healing is not always obvious. Sometimes, it shows up in moments we'd rather ignore, when we're too busy, too responsible, or too conditioned to ask for help. I thought I understood what it meant to use my voice, to advocate for myself. But one moment, tucked inside a painful week and an unexpected urgent care visit, revealed how healing often starts...with one quiet decision to be seen.

Healing is available to us at all times. We just need the awareness to receive it. Then it unfolds as we make active choices to witness, act, and learn from our experiences. I was well into my exploration of self-acceptance and inner child healing when I experienced a major catharsis. It was so unexpected, and it left me quite stunned. I was actively exploring what it meant to use my voice more intentionally. Immediately, my mind aligned with speaking up, using my voice to advocate for myself, and leaning more deeply into the full truth. I did not make a deep connection with the act of asking for and receiving help as part of that work, but I learned quickly that they are inexplicably tied.

The night before a week-long business trip, I began to feel very tired and lethargic. I noticed that I was having some pain in my lower back and pelvic area. While it was noticeable, I continued to pack and prepare myself for bed. Early the next morning, I woke up to go to the bathroom and was in significant pain. My body was so stiff that it took a few minutes to navigate the pain while rolling over to get out of bed. When I returned to bed, I prayed and asked for strength and healing while I slept.

At the sound of my alarm, I rolled over with the same level of difficulty as earlier and about the same amount of pain. I decided to do a quick assessment of what I thought might be wrong with the resources available to me, take some medicine I had on hand, and then head to the airport. It was a pretty uncomfortable cross-country flight, but I was clear that I was actively healing and had no intention of not being present and fully active for my engagement.

I navigated through the half-day prep session with increasing pain. After dinner, I was so grateful to be able to get into bed. I quickly found that it was difficult to find a comfortable position to sleep in, and that getting up overnight to use the bathroom was even more challenging. The next morning, I was in even more pain. It took a few minutes to get out of bed and grab my slippers to head to the bathroom. I started praying as I got into the shower and very quickly heard, "Urgent Care." I brushed off the nudge and finished my shower. Just as I was exiting the shower, I reconsidered. I started running through the plan for the day. I had a few hours open before I needed to be on site and a couple of additional hours before the start of my session. I waffled back and forth, mostly wasting time and frustrating myself with indecision. Finally, I decided to go to urgent care right away, with the hope that I would be back in more than enough time. While I was getting ready, I listened to a few messages. My friend left a voice message the evening before, encouraging me to go to urgent care. It was confirmation. I booked an appointment quickly, and within minutes, I was in the Uber.

I completed the virtual check-in on my way to the appointment. When I arrived, I was informed that I was at the right provider but at the wrong location. I used maps to find the urgent care and then used the location to open the website. Given my unfamiliarity with the location, I thought that the appointment was at the exact location I selected. The new location was about 20 minutes away, and my appointment was scheduled to start in 5 minutes. Much of the next few minutes went by at warp speed.

"Unfortunately, we only take scheduled appointments at this location, no walk-ins," said the receptionist.

"But I do have an appointment, just not here," I said quietly.

"We wish we could help you, but we are fully booked. There is no way the doctor will have space to see you," responded the PA, who was actively scouring the schedule.

Tears started to flow gently. I was wiping them quickly as I tried to answer quick questions about what brought me in. I must have told them that I was from out of town, experiencing a lot of pain, and other details, because I remember them recounting those things to me later in my visit. What I remember clearly is what happened next.

"Ma'am, we can call the other location and let them know that you are on your way and ask them to please hold your appointment time so you don't have to go into their walk-in queue. Would you like us to do that?" As I nodded, I could not stop the flow of tears rushing down my face. I turned away from the desk and walked towards the back of the waiting room, where there was a box of tissues. After a few long strides to reach the box, I started to sob aloud. As my breathing quickened, I realized that I was hyperventilating. I was reminding myself to breathe as I cried. I can only imagine their faces as they watched me literally fall apart.

Perhaps it was the thought of them seeing me folding into the pain and sadness. Maybe it was the clock ticking in my head, reminding me that I didn't have much time before my work engagement would need to begin. Something moved in me. I cleared my throat, gathered my composure as I had done countless times before in my life, and turned around. I walked back to the counter. With my phone in one hand and a tissue underneath it, I asked the receptionist if he would please give me the address of the new location. I had my Uber app open and started entering the information to request a car.

The PA interjected," What I can do while you are here is take a urine sample. I can't guarantee which site will support you, but at least we can initiate the process. Would you like me to do that for you?"

"Yes, please." It was all I could muster in the moment.

I followed her back to an exam room as she prepared the sample I needed to complete. Tears were flowing the entire time. After the sample, I was led back to the exam room to wait. The PA appeared again. "You mentioned that you were in a lot of pain. I have a shot that I can administer to provide relief for several hours. Would you like me to get that set up for you?" "Yes, please." I smiled, and the tears started again. Somehow, I knew at that moment that I was about 7 or 8 years old again. The rest of the experience was top-notch. There was a cancellation, so the provider was able to see me, as was their assistant. They confirmed my self-diagnosis and let me know they were sending the sample to the lab. I'm certain there are other pieces I've missed, but I was centered in the moment in a way that was simply different.

"They saw me. I allowed myself to be seen, and they took care of me," I shared with my mom. I tried to hide the pain, my tears, and the angst, but I let it all be seen. Because I chose to allow myself to be seen, I put myself in the position to have the support I needed. God showed up in a big way in that moment.

In the weeks prior, I was working on healing my aversion to asking for help. I have such joy in helping others, but I often avoid asking for and accepting help. Of course, I had not understood the root or what it indicated across the decades of my life. I was that way for as long as I can remember. It wasn't always pleasant. I definitely wrestled with resentment and the feeling of being taken advantage of as a result of my missing unenforced boundaries. In God's process of helping me heal, I had this very specific experience. It brought my desire to please others to center stage. I began by prioritizing work over my health without considering how I could balance both. I fought back those tears because I didn't want to be a burden or a spectacle. What was wrong with allowing myself to cry in a public place anyway?

As I stood in the back of the waiting room, I felt the pain for the first time. Since waking up the morning before, I had been tucking the pain away and telling myself it wasn't that bad. The pain was easily a seven on a 10-point scale. It was not good, yet I kept trying to pretend I wasn't hurting. I actually did not know how to just say, "Please take care of me, I need help." It was a phrase I had swallowed thousands of times before, deciding to sidestep the disappointment of others choosing themselves first despite my attempts to squeeze them into my overflowing calendars or rearrange plans to suit them. Yes, this moment brought so many of the healing lessons of the last few years into view. The bow tied around it all was choice. It was time for me to choose to take care of myself. It was ok to allow myself to be seen.

My inner child was so pleased with how they took care of me. I was so pleased with how I took care of myself.

The pain medicine was expected to kick in within an hour or two. It was at least 4 hours before I felt relief. It indicated how much pain I was truly capable of carrying and how I had been tucking it away so much that I really didn't realize what I was experiencing. As I rested that afternoon, still navigating the discomfort and pain, God was very present. They brought my attention back to the moments and experiences of the morning, as well as some prominent times across my life where I wanted help but didn't ask. They showed me moments when people wanted to help, and I turned them away. I saw moments where I was desperate to be seen in the way I can so effortlessly see others, more often than not. Then God showed me moments where They sent people to support me and the myriad of ways I responded. I finally got it. Today was different because I allowed myself to be seen and to ask for help. Over the following few days, I received healing during my morning prayer and meditation. I saw myself releasing old beliefs and choosing to embody what I know and who I truly am. I was healing, and God had orchestrated it all in response to my petition to be a better version of myself. All healing comes from God.

If you find the notion of your being responsible for the place you are in your healing journey disturbing, place your bookmark here and step away. Return to the book when your curious desire brings you back to seeking truth. If you are not ready for the truth, that's okay. Accept that you are where you are today, and return when you are ready. It is important to note that you will not always be ready for the truth when it is presented. Sometimes, you need to see and hear the truth multiple times before it resonates. That is the beauty of having this book. You can read it again as many times as you like.

Try reading through this chapter first thing in the morning. Your likelihood of being open to receiving is stronger as you start your day. Make time to journal about how you feel right now. Those who willingly accept this truth may also find that journaling brings some perspectives to light that they are unaware of. Awareness of your feelings and responses is a part of the healing process. You deserve to take this moment to see yourself.

Now that you are ready to proceed, healing will greet you. Your readiness to heal begins with accepting accountability for where you are today. Where you are today is good. It is a blessing. This moment holds great promise and potential. You get to make the next move. The decision is in your hands. You have made it to this point in your life and have chosen to consider your healing journey. Celebrate the choices that have led you to this moment. There is no need to dwell on the past and curse the things that have happened. They have all been used to help you progress to this moment. Your journey consists of the learnings and experiences, as evidenced in the preceding chapters. At this moment, you have done what you needed to do to move through the past and be here now. Welcome to the promise of today. Today, you can choose to delve deep into the healing that is required to emerge as your whole self.

All healing comes from the creator. It is divine. Your healing journey is deeply personal, and while you play a vital role in it, true healing ultimately comes from the Creator. Recognizing that complete healing cannot occur without the divine is essential. How can one heal without the connection to what the full self is intended to be? You need an understanding of the self to heal to that form. For example, if you see three pieces of string lying parallel to each other and are told that they are the sides of a shape, how do you know what shape to make? Could it be that they make a triangle? Perhaps they are for a square or rectangle, and you will be given another piece. With three more pieces of string, you could have a hexagon. In essence, you will never know if you are putting the pieces together correctly unless you understand what you are creating.

Take the exercise a step further. Some of you may have decided, 'I would make a triangle anyway. I would use what I have and make the best guess.' Others would seek more information and perhaps refuse to move until more clarity was available. Still, others would become enraged and decide it was a waste of time. They would likely choose to ignore it altogether. If you see yourself in one of these scenarios or would choose something entirely different, it does not matter. It is simply an opportunity to see yourself and your default reaction to situations. Regardless of the reaction and subsequent choices you would have made in this scenario, you are right. Yes, you are right. Go ahead and exhale. Often, you long to hear that statement, and here it is. You are right. At this moment, you didn't have enough information to be sure of what was expected, so you did what you knew how to do. You are right because you chose what was best for you, based on comfort, experience, desire, or any other rationale you brought to this moment. It is well.

Now, consider how this exercise relates to healing. You bring the same perspective and default behavior to healing. It is okay. It is what you were taught to do and what you saw modeled for you. This approach is prevalent across many industries and practices, where seeking the root cause or underlying conditions is not the initial step. Your world has become a place where everything is sought with an instant response—an immediate action.

Teaching the practice of gazing at a challenge and thinking about an approach is limited. It is not honored in practice. Gazing at a challenge is a bit like chess. There is a plan in the player's mind, an assumption of what they would do next. Once their opponent moves, they may gaze for a bit. Even if they know which move is suitable for this moment, they may want to consider the next few scenarios. We can see the benefit of examining the situation or problem from multiple angles. Often, time helps clarify your vision.

Think of the last time you went to see a physician. You likely expected an immediate answer about what caused the condition that brought you in. When the physician says, "I'm not certain, so we should run a few tests," the response is often one of disdain. The value of immediacy and action has replaced the value of certainty and clarity. You want the doctor to know right away and to be sure. You are looking for an immediate plan of action. That plan is what you perceive as the conduit to experiencing peace. As you consider this perspective, you begin to see the paradox.

Peace does not come from another human. It is found within yourself as a divine gift. It is always present, regardless of circumstances. You were born with peace. You knew how to return to peace whenever you desired. As you received a release of conditions you desired to change, a dirty diaper, or the need to burp, peace returned. At times, when another human resolved the condition, you may not have chosen peace. You may have continued to cry or to be restless because their act of caring for you could not give you peace. As you have grown older, you have forgotten that this is how things work. *You are peace.* You have peace because it is within you as a part of your divinity. It is always within your reach, and the opportunity to choose peace is constant. Humanity continually searches for peace. The search is misplaced when you look for it to come from sources other than yourself.

When you look to the relief of certain stimuli as the thing that will give you peace, you relinquish your personal power. You are tapped into the energy of man that is grounded in ego. Ego says, "There is something that will fix me. You (my doctor) have it, and I demand that you fix it." Ego also lends itself to the belief that because of the doctor's education and experience, they are the most capable of resolving your complaint. You are willing to relinquish your knowledge of self to someone else based solely on factors outside of yourself. There is a clear experiential and educational advantage that your doctor has. The years of extensive training, ongoing learning, and repeated practice with patients make them incredibly knowledgeable. However, relying on your doctor for all the answers and expecting them to be instantaneous is an erroneous expectation. In the best scenarios, the doctor should be given two things you can offer- time and you.

It is true that many things can be diagnosed quickly and treated almost immediately. It is likely that you arrived with a hypothesis and lots of information to help the doctor assess things quickly. In situations where you arrive with a more vague and broad set of symptoms, it would make sense to offer the physician more time to determine the potential root cause and to establish the course of treatment. Those situations are more emotionally charged, and people are less open to giving time for assessment, even though the most thorough diagnosis would provide the best treatment path.

Even those who do not often visit the doctor may arrive without a comprehensive list of their symptoms. This presents the second issue of expecting certainty from someone outside of yourself. Critical information is lost when details are not shared with the doctor. Each symptom is data. The frequency of occurrence, corresponding symptoms, and any other relevant information you can provide will help identify potential causes of the issue. Without the information, time is lost, and depending on the issue, certainty may not be achieved. The ideal scenario is to view yourself as responsible and to gather as much information as possible to support the physician in fulfilling their role. Noting symptoms and conditions while engaging the doctor as a partner is a necessary shift.

You are at the core of this equation. Healing is your responsibility to yourself and the collective. As you read in the last chapter, you are not alone in your existence. Your physical, emotional, mental, and spiritual conditions have an impact on those around you as much as it does on yourself. The interaction with others is a part of existing in the world. There is interconnectedness in your energy from one to another. The behavior and mindsets of each person have the potential to impact others through interaction and presence. The connection between one and another means that conditions, whether healed or unhealed, will inevitably affect others. You deserve to heal. Your journey to heal will have a halo on the collective, but most importantly, you will heal yourself.

Healing yourself does not mean that you do not require support on your journey. Ideally, each person would have a "team" of people engaged in their healing journey. You may assemble your team in a traditional way with physicians or design a more holistic team. Your team's composition should reflect the support you require for your healing journey. It is important to see yourself as the leader of that team. Each team member should understand the areas in which you are focused on healing across physical, emotional, mental, and spiritual dimensions. Your mindset will be reset by seeing yourself as ultimately accountable for your healing. This is a good time to pause and reflect on how you want to shift your healing journey. Envision yourself leading the healing process. What does it feel like to take the reins? How do you imagine yourself showing up differently with your healthcare providers and other healing partners? What will you do differently in this moment to truly allow yourself to move into a position to heal yourself? Enjoy the revelations and commitments you capture as you take time to journal.

Tapping into healing requires a determination of who is leading the work. It will be difficult to experience deep and sustaining change without your commitment to the subject. Sometimes, you may feel conflicted about healing. The current situation may be comfortable for you; therefore, you may not desire the healing that surpasses the certainty you have today. In times when you feel the current level of healing is sufficient, allow yourself grace for a time. Instead of focusing on actions towards healing, allow yourself to center on your why. Reflect on your progress and why it mattered to you to get to where you are. Allow yourself to explore the other things you want to achieve in life, not limited to activities, but to include who you are choosing to be in this life. Thinking of our potential impact and connectivity to others can be incredibly compelling. As you lean into connection, your energy begins to shift. By allowing yourself to see what is possible without the intense self-applied pressure to act, you will be drawn to continue doing the work.

Momentum is very important and incredibly valuable in sustaining changed behavior. While that is seemingly accurate, the unique place of healing requires something different. Many ways people are motivated and inspired are less effective when they focus on healing. "Grace and pace applied with love" will keep a person in a space of healing. It is the grace and love that is poured into self that encourages loving behavior to become the new normal. To effectively break a cycle not grounded in love, one must apply love. Love encourages acceptance, rest, understanding, and a varied pace based solely on the individual's plight.

Through love, an environment that welcomes change will be designed. Perspective will evolve and help to heal damaged places in a person's relationship with change. Change is inherently good as it creates the necessary conditions for the cycles of life. The processes or experiences attached to change are not always pleasant, but they are essential to growth.

You can heal. You can tap into healing for yourself! You were created with what you need and the capability to heal. This is a freeing statement. The ability to heal is present in every human. Hopefully, you feel excited by the fact that the ability is already present within you. Support is available to you across multiple disciplines through practitioners who tap into the varied aspects of healing across the dimensions within you.

Physicians support your physical and mental dimensions, while you might engage in therapy to support your mental and emotional dimensions. Focusing on the spiritual dimension may connect you with spiritual and religious leaders or spiritual practices, such as prayer and meditation. The dimensions are linked, so work in one area or with a practitioner may overlap into other areas. The overlap is a good thing. Inner child work is extremely powerful, as so many answers await us in childhood introspection. Behavioral patterns like coping, self-soothing, trauma responses, and more were established in our youth. While they may present differently in adulthood, some threads connect back to your youth. Finding an expert practitioner or methodology that helps you reconnect and address childhood wounds is highly beneficial. As you begin to identify what you want to address, think broadly. You are a whole person; the more you can incorporate solutions that consider all aspects of the issue, the more effective the treatment will be.

Behavioral Coach

One of the best experiences I've had is working with a behavioral coach. As a part of a program preparing me to return to work after a leave of absence, I was connected with a therapist and a behavioral coach. I was very familiar with therapy, but needed clarification about the benefits of the coach. The behavioral coach I was connected with was phenomenal. In addition to the depth of knowledge of the body, various practices, and coaching expertise, she shared my religious beliefs. A consummate professional, she waited until I shared some of my deep understanding of who God created me to be and the importance of living into my purpose. Over time, she was able to connect practices to my faith and the desires that I have for my life. She taught me ways to observe myself and practices for managing stress and anxiety. She understood the desire to self-sacrifice in a way that was incredibly validating; she was also able to point me to scripture and stories that helped me reflect on my behavior in ways that were different.

My therapist also shared my spiritual beliefs and had a deep understanding of many of the complexities I was experiencing as I underwent several critical changes in my life. The combination of my behavioral coach, therapist, and daily practices of meditation and prayer significantly aided my healing journey. Each one did something different but related to my healing journey. Individually, each practice would have made an impact. Together, we were able to make significant strides in my healing. The insights and introspection were the most powerful outcomes. I took what we worked on in the sessions back to God in prayer. I journaled and shared insights with my coach and therapist. There was a connected view of what would be most supportive as I returned to work. It was incredibly powerful, preparing me for that transition and deepening my core confidence that I was ready for who I was emerging into being.

Therapy offers many modalities that can support a patient in their healing journey. In addition, the therapist's beliefs and practices can be beneficial for creating an even deeper connection with their client. Consider a therapist who shares the same spiritual beliefs as their client. They are able to understand the client's perspectives and connect with the client's beliefs in a way that supports multiple areas of the client's life. This does not suggest that someone with a different perspective is less effective. It is quite the contrary. Different perspectives and the opportunity to engage in self-exploration are a core part of therapy.

What is worth exploring is the way that a practitioner can help the client explore multiple sides of themselves. The places of connection often create a shared language and understanding that can deepen the client's progress. Sharing experiences and understanding can help the client in their self-exploration. Another benefit is the recommendation of practices aligned with the client's beliefs.

Consider yourself the CHO- Chief Healing Officer, chosen by you and entrusted to orchestrate and sometimes facilitate your own healing. As the CHO, your work is to convene a team of practitioners to review your case. To lead the discussion and determine the best course of action, you need to be well-versed in the current status of the patient, as well as your own. Tapping into healing begins when you look within to understand what is happening in your body's systems, within your mind, and emotionally, as well as by examining your spiritual connection. While there are other components, we will focus on these four explicitly.

Healing is rarely one-dimensional. While practical support systems and therapeutic tools are critical, spiritual alignment often becomes the turning point. Once I had the right people around me, I also had to acknowledge and deal with the truth within me. That's where the deeper work began.

Spiritual

Most of humanity is spiritually sick. There is a deep fog over the spiritual truths you were born knowing. You have access to all of the truth, yet it feels safer to stay in a prison of your own making. The world around you does not make it easy to delve deeper into your own knowledge. Like the world around you, the brain focuses on stability and certainty. Certainty is grounded in what you know to be true already. It can be a perceived positive or negative situation, as long as you know what to make of it- that is certainty. The inner conflict arises when you desire truth but choose to remain in a state of sameness. You know the truth; when you are ready, you will open yourself to access it.

When spiritual healing is considered, one must address the things often dismissed. Begin by redefining Spirituality as separate from religion. Let go of the rigid walls that encourage you to stay small and embrace the limiting beliefs you have been taught. Spirit is expansive, God is expansive, and therefore, you are expansive. Spirituality is suffering because people choose routine and acceptance over truth. Your spirituality calls you forward

into your knowing and relationship with your Creator. As you
ground yourself in deep truth, the space for you to grow and
know more expands. This is ongoing throughout your life. When
you are grounded in your spirituality, you begin to question the
paradigms and truths you have been taught. The curiosity that
connects to spirituality is transformative. This quest for truth is
a traveling companion with your journey of purpose. Both lead
you deeper into an intimate relationship with God.

Tapping In

During the heart of my inner child healing work, I enlisted the support
of an expert Inner Child Healing Coach. We identified a general course
of action, and she guided me comfortably through an exploration that
ultimately led to healing the relationship between my inner child and
my current adult self. As a practitioner, I knew that many answers
emerged in childhood, as I was very aware of the traumas I experienced. I recognized that patterns like retreating into my ice castle
were a part of the way I believed that I was keeping myself safe. I
was unaware that my adolescent self was stuck in a particular stage of
development. As I learned more about how our responses often mimic
the typical response of someone at the age where a trauma occurred,
I began to notice the behavior and connect the response to what may
have been the catalyst. What I didn't realize was that my adolescent self
had created a way to navigate that looked more mature while actually
internalizing emotion. It seemed that she was well adjusted, but in
truth, she had become a master at swallowing emotion.

She was stuck, abandoned really, in a particular moment that seemingly had no real significance to me in my adulthood. During the healing work, I learned how incredibly exhausted she was. I had silenced her, deciding that I did not want to deal with the truths that she carried. I did not know how to reconnect with her. My coach helped me learn to trust myself and reconnect with her, ultimately building a healthy relationship. I did not know how critical it was to my healing journey, but I realized later that self-acceptance was at the heart of my healing process during this time. Self-acceptance is the gift I gave myself that allowed my gifts to really grow, and opened me up to the wisdom that I carry. It created continuity and peace within me, which we often refer to as alignment.

Perhaps my favorite example of the impact of self-acceptance happened during a healing journey. I would often receive, in the moment, information that helped me advise others on how to heal. For example, someone might mention a recurring issue, and almost immediately, a particular herb or remedy would come to mind. If I were unfamiliar with the remedy or the issue, I was incredibly skeptical of what I was receiving. My next step was to pray for clarity about this remedy before sharing it. I also referenced books to see if my remedy aligned. I cannot remember an occasion when it did not. As you might imagine, I still found it hard to believe until I experienced my "knowing" during the journey. At some point, I remember tapping healing affirmations into my body. I began to repeat something very specific that was geared to embed truth and awareness of wisdom. I thought that my coach had taught me to do it, and I was shocked to learn that she had not given me instructions on what to do or the words to use. I was clear that what I was doing was working as I began to feel the truth permeate my being. I was experiencing what I said.

As I continued on my journey and received divine messages, I began to understand the healing wisdom that I carry more deeply.

After the journey, I asked my coach more about the tapping. I was familiar with the practice of tapping, but never really took to the practice. It was clear that I knew what to do and how to do it. My coach said, "It was clear that you knew exactly what to do. You knew how to heal yourself." I was stunned. During the journey, I was healing myself and reconnecting to my divinity. I needed to heal the wounded relationship with my inner child in order to trust myself to open the pathway to healing. I knew what to do and was learning to trust myself again, which occurred through self-acceptance. Tapping into healing is literal and figurative. You have the ability to utilize self-healing practices like tapping to support you on your journey. In order to trust the capacity you have for your own healing, you must have a higher level of trust in yourself to surpass the conditioning that discourages you as a safety mechanism. You may know that you are capable, but believing it is connected to your self-acceptance.

Chapter Pearls

- All healing comes from God. You have a choice about whether or not you engage in your own healing as of this moment. Give yourself grace for the past when you were unaware of the access you had to your own healing.

- Peace is found within you, and it cannot be given to you by another person.

- You are the CHO. You can heal yourself. With the gifts that God has given you, healing is yours to engage in when you choose.

Journal Prompts

- The acknowledgment that you are responsible for healing and that you have had what you needed is a deep truth. Journal about how you felt reading this truth. Was it easy to offer yourself grace for not addressing healing sooner?

- What is your first action as the newly appointed CHO- Chief Healing Officer of your life?

Chapter Five

Getting Started

How do you heal? That question is part of the foundation of the work that must be done to heal. Many steps, protocols, and methodologies can be involved in healing. We refer to many of these as modalities. Modalities typically refer to methods or specific processes that are enlisted as a practice to support healing. We will use this as the general understanding of "processes" throughout this chapter.

Healing is a process. In and of itself, healing takes time and has many stages. There are many reasons for the complexity of healing. Most simply, healing requires the examination of multiple vantage points to understand what needs to be healed. We carry information in our DNA, create patterns based on experiences, compare ourselves to others, and have learned behaviors to contend with. These are just a few examples of what contributes to the environment within that contributes to the need for healing.

Past experiences and traumas inform our perspectives and responses to similar conditions, adding another layer of depth to the need for healing. When we experience similar stimuli, there is a compounding effect; the brain reinforces the message around the conditions, making us interpret conditions in a similar way. The more we perceive and respond similarly, the more we reinforce that pattern.

To simplify this concept, first, we identify why we want to heal. Our next step is to determine what we want to heal. We support that decision with the selection of the methods we will use to heal. Processes are the "what," and actions refer to "how" you choose to utilize the process in your healing journey. They are connected, but they are not the same. This chapter will explore the connection between why we heal and how we heal. The "What of Healing" explores the methods one can employ in one's healing journey. This chapter is about the linkage of methods to why we heal. This is important to determine first. If we were to move straight into action, those steps might be misaligned with the ultimate goal of our healing. We need to understand the why to know what we want to do to address it. The genesis of action starts with knowing the why. By now, you realize that so much of what you do is driven by external factors. This is part of rewiring behavior: looking at the reason first and then determining what is based on your circumstances and desired outcomes.

The list is incredibly long; you can find resources in the book's upcoming sections. Yes, the "how" matters, but you can't appropriately select the "how" without knowing what you are healing and why. Let's start with understanding some of the processes. Actionable steps will be addressed in a later chapter.

You might ask now, What do you do to heal? The processes by which you heal may feel overwhelming. That is to be expected. Healing is a journey and will have its complexities. In the same way that it took time to evolve into the current state, it will take time to heal. The beauty of the journey is that it does become more comfortable, and perhaps easier for some, as you continue to do the work. When you understand what you are doing, it should give you a sense of calm and peace. Healing is about aligning with your body, emotions, mindset, and spirituality, connecting with the body in its original state.

You might find yourself yearning for the answers. "What do I do to heal?" "How do I heal?" Understand that the first step is to begin at the surface with what you know needs healing and what you are willing to heal. Allow yourself to let go of the other questions for a moment. Yes, you want to heal and will when you are ready to do the work. Often, people make things more complex by focusing on the process rather than allowing it to evolve around the intentions that we set. It will help you understand how to go about your healing work and begin to visualize where you want to start. Understand that there is no "right or wrong" place to start. What matters is that you start. It is beneficial to begin in a place where you feel inspired to create healing progress in your life.

If you find yourself brimming with energy to get started, this would be a great time to journal. Think about what feels urgent to address in your healing. What is driving your current excitement to heal? What do you hope to gain or see as you begin your healing journey? What are you most curious to explore? What questions do you want to answer about your path to healing as you finish this and the book's subsequent chapters?

Energy

Perhaps the best place to start is with an understanding of energy. Many processes that help us heal address energy in and around the body. We are energy. Our bodies are made of energy, and we transform energy through our thoughts, actions, and words. Every thought is filled with energy. Our intentions, which are often defined as an idea and the decision to do something about that idea, are filled with energy. The world and everything within it is energy.

Let us explore thoughts. Dr. Ralph Lewis states, "A thought is a representation of something." In his article, he describes that thoughts represent or provide "A likeness—a thing that depicts another thing by having characteristics that correspond to that other thing." This helps us acknowledge that what is and what has the potential to be can impact us in our healing journey. Because you can hold a vision for yourself as true, the brain cannot independently tell the difference between what is and what is possible. Thoughts, filled with energy, can and do form reality around you. That reality shifts in moments when you may not be fully aware.

Perhaps you are aware of someone who is a self-identified over-thinker. They must identify it themselves, as no one else can ever truly know how much time is spent in the mind of another. That person likely describes contemplating the various options of what might happen, likely responses, and subsequent responses, followed by how everyone might feel. They discard scenarios as they return to the initial thought and eventually choose a course of action. Imagine in your mind's eye that the world around you was responding to every idea in their contemplation. If we truly believe in the definition of energy, that thought has to go somewhere. It is reasonable to think that the thought, carrying possibilities, consumes an energetic conversation with the divine, pulling on the possibilities of a potential outcome.

Using your imagination, see a tiny army of "energy responders," a team of energetic laborers whose only mission is to solve the challenges you are working through. It is easy to envision the overthinking process becoming a constant start-stop-pause-resume cycle of responding to the overthinking. A real-life example might resemble the initial stages of building a house. Imagine if, every two days or so, the architect made structural changes to the design of the house. The exhaustion of the construction team would be evident. Every change would risk elements of the timeline, permits, and availability of materials.

Journey back to the image of this tiny army of responders. How confused might they be when a perfectly plausible plan is identified and discarded without clarity? When overthinking happens, it is our overactive protective instincts that spring into action. Something unhealed within makes the person continuously plan scenarios to reduce risk. There are numerous benefits to exploring this topic. The energy expended in overthinking is precious energy that can be redirected to taking action. It can be used to recenter or calm the swelling of anxious energy inside. The more patterns can be observed and disturbed, the more transparent the case for healing.

One of the best ways to address overthinking is to write. Take a moment to write the problem down. Instead of capturing scenarios and talking points, write down why having multiple plans for this situation is essential. Ask yourself what would happen if you committed to one course of action and let go of the potential questions that might arise. What would you gain? What would you lose?

By challenging yourself to observe your behavior and explore your why, you can delve deeper into the case for healing. This begs the question, "What are you protecting?" By answering that question, you will open the door to a beautiful understanding of your motivations. Be gentle with yourself. This kind of insight is required to lead your healing.

Begin this part of your healing journey with a renewed sense of openness. Decide to embrace grace as your partner on the journey. Often, people resort to the idea that they "should have known" when things are presented to them. Ground yourself in the truth that you didn't know it all. It is important to remember that you learn things over time. Even though answers may have been within, they were not actively in your awareness; You needed to have the experience of trusting yourself to allow the emergence of healing insight to be realized. Consider this a new chapter in your healing. You may have faced challenges in the past that you are now fully equipped to handle. Trusting yourself is the key. Link your desire to heal with the knowledge that you can do this work, and you will.

This brings back the question of what is important about energy. Since energy exists and cannot be created or destroyed, it is always present. You get to direct energy towards what matters to you. All too often, people are not aware of where they are spending their energy. Overthinking is not where energy is best spent. It is wasted on worst-case scenario planning ad nauseam because simply spending time envisioning what could happen plants those possibilities as credible in our minds. The work here is to focus on clarifying what is really desired. What experiences are meaningful and will foster growth and healing? How might you counter the old constructs of your mind with new ones that open you up to possibilities? That is both the journey of life and the pathway to healing.

Incorporating God

As we've already established, all healing comes from God. One of the most important things you can do during your healing journey is to start with God. Pray, seek, and converse with The Divine. Your healing journey is about your relationship with your Creator and self. This happens best when you look for God's direction and instruction on where to focus on your healing. God will help you know what needs to be healed by helping you to see yourself. You can expect God to communicate with you in whatever ways you are open. They will provide insight when you seek divine wisdom. If you are attentive to dreams, you may begin to see patterns or themes show up in the dreams that you remember. Some of you may be tuned into your hearing of God, so you may hear God speak to you about the areas of focus for your healing journey. Alternatively, your messages may come through other people.

You might see patterns coming to the forefront of your awareness. Often, it happens with behavioral patterns that have been there for as long as you can remember, but they are so commonplace that they haven't captured your attention in the past. But now, simply because you've come to God with a genuine desire to begin to heal, you will begin to see yourself. The patterns become more visible. You begin to see the destructive impacts of some old patterns. There is more insight about what is happening inside of you and in your relationships with others. God is gracefully showing you that the truth is the best place to start.

When you commit to being open, you will inevitably experience an openness in others to help you see yourself. We can choose to remember that before we were here, there was a purpose offered to each of us. Part of our journey includes helping others experience themselves and God's love. Remember that there are people in your life designed to help you see yourself. Because healing is relational, you can ask others for their reflections back to you in relation to what God has shown you. Just be careful not to weigh their opinions or perspectives more heavily than your own or the weight that God assigns to you.

It is also helpful to remember that quite often, people don't want things to change in you because of the impact it has on them and their experience of you. They would much rather things stay familiar, as we've read in earlier chapters. So, if you're looking for perspective from others, ensure you're asking for confirmation of what you already know or believe. Ask specifically for examples of not just the behavior but of the impact. Compare the impact they recount to what you know and have experienced through your own reflection.

Reviewing the impact is critical. It will help inform you about what needs to be addressed and offer insight for inclusion in envisioning what you want in future relationships. For example, if you stop to ask questions like, "What would be different if I did things this way...?" you will begin to broaden your perspective. Eventually, you will see shifts that can help you further identify how things can evolve to facilitate your healing. Seeing these shifts happen is a way for you to document the changes in your healing journey and to become more and more comfortable with the shifts that you are experiencing. When you invite God in, it will happen in ways that will most certainly help you to become all of who you were created to be.

As you might imagine, the revelation of patterns may not always be pleasant. Having a willingness to see yourself and clarity about why this is the right time to heal are essential, but they may not soften the blow of receiving the insight you need to heal. Real healing includes sitting with uncomfortable feelings and new insights. During this process, you learn to extend more grace to yourself, employ forgiveness, and develop more empathy for others. There is significant growth that happens during the discomfort. Try to remember that all of the process is important and has an impact on who you are choosing to become.

GOD, Show Me Me

My ongoing prayer is, "God, show me, me." I say it daily. I ask it humbly and purely. I have shared this phrase hundreds of times. I feel immense joy when others include it in their prayers and when I am blessed to hear the testimonies that include their use of my prayer point. It is a part of how I move through the world. It wasn't always easy, though. In fact, I actually wanted the opposite most of the time.

In the early stages of my walk with God, I was intensely focused on getting everything right. A desire for validation heavily influenced my approach to life, as I sought approval from my parents, friends, sorors, and colleagues. This need for acceptance was deeply rooted in my pursuit of approval. I was a gymnast of sorts. I bent and flexed myself to the will of others regularly. I had some level of interest in seeing myself, but more so from the desire for validation that I was enough, doing enough, or giving enough. In retrospect, I wonder how many hours of sleep I gave up worrying about others or my decisions, and how it would impact everyone I knew. I felt guilty when I couldn't "do more," even if what I had already given was exhaustive of what should have been reasonably provided. I poured out energy until I was depleted. I showed up everywhere, even though I was too tired to go. I answered the late-night calls that made me tired at work the next day. All of these patterns were regularly in place in my teens and 20s. So, in truth, I did not want God to reveal myself to me. I was reasonably sure that God would make me change, which meant I would be on a journey to disappoint others. That was simply not what I had designed for who I was around.

Of course, I would inevitably have to change and embrace God's desires. I was deep into my walk a few years ago after evolving into who God designed me to be. I was less connected to the validation of others. I had begun asking God regularly to show me myself and openly receiving the response. In most cases, even when I did not want what God showed me to be true, I embraced it. It became more important to me to become who God called me to be than to hold on to the old versions of self. Certainly, there were moments when I did not like what I saw, but I held on to the truth that I was doing my best as I evolved that part of my way of being, and that now that I could see it, I could change it. It helped me to let go and allow myself grace.

Then, one day, God shook me during a call with my mentor, sister-friend, and prophetic voice. She is an incredible light and divine advisor. How God has worked through our relationship has helped change my life. I honor God's light in her. When God has an intense message, it often comes through her as a reminder or confirmation. I was not surprised at the message coming through her, as she is a trusted confidant and powerful vessel of God's love. It was the message that shocked me the most. The content of the conversation was varied. We were close to the end of the call when she said, "You know if you are not able to access your heart fully, you will not be able to fulfill your mission for God." I was stunned. I don't remember my response. I am relatively sure that I said something like " I am." or something to help me hold on to the part of my identity that felt suddenly wobbly. "What did that mean, and why hadn't God told me that directly?"

I went to God in prayer. It took a moment after the call to gather my thoughts. In truth, being connected to my heart is my work. Whatever God has called me to do and who I am is rooted in my heart, being fully connected to God. I carry something precious to God, which lives in my heart. How could it be possible that I wasn't fully accessing my heart?

Healing happens when we are willing to see ourselves. I did not want it to be true. I wanted to be misunderstood or not fully seen, which would have made it someone else's issue, not mine. Fortunately for me, God is so brilliant that they sent one of the few people who unequivocally never had an agenda with me. She knows my heart on a spiritual level and works with me regularly. Trusted by me and God, she came to say exactly what God said through her. It did not matter if she experienced it or not. God trusted her to say it as it was said to her. What was even better is that she had insight and examples if I needed them. She could share that there were times when she observed me holding back. The words spoke deeply to something that resonated. *I knew it was true, but didn't know how to fix it.*

In times past, I would have asked questions to "make it better for the other person and their experience of me." In this case, that substitute was not appropriate. She was not connected to my response or actions beyond the genuine love for me to become all God placed within me. I've reflected on the moment many times with such gratitude. I heard what God needed me to hear, and I didn't have an answer without returning to Them.

I went to God in prayer and started by surrendering my self-perception to God's perspective. "I've asked you to show me me, and you have. Help me to see it in real-time, to understand how it makes others feel, and show me how you desire it to be in me." My openness to feedback and regular surrender opened the floodgates for feedback, examples, and opportunities to test and learn. Understanding how to connect with my heart has become a lifelong journey. It's my mission to master this skill as I evolve and to guide others along the way.

The other valuable lesson that emerged is that we are in a constant state of evolution. I wanted to have "arrived" at who God created me to be. Instead, I was growing into what was required for this season. The next season would require more work on my heart connection, and so forth.

Hopefully, you are interested in what I learned and why I had to learn it. It was pretty simple in words and complex in reality. I had to learn how to be more vulnerable with others. I had to choose to stop being performative. I had to decide to remove my mask. I was masterful at creating places for other people to feel safe and to be vulnerable. It was God's gift working through me. What was difficult for me was being vulnerable enough to hold space without offering answers or solutions. It felt vulnerable to just offer to hold space and to allow the emotional connection to be all that is, while the person works to create their solution. Part of my role is to create the space for them to be in communion with God so that they connect directly rather than through my human explanation of things. I was being directed to explore why I still felt unworthy. I learned I could experience joy and peace amidst people I loved who were in pain and discomfort. I believed in the past that I had to experience the same thing that they were going through. That wasn't true at all. I learned that God's desire for me was to allow unconditional love to SHOW through, even in times of dismay and disappointment.

One of the greatest lessons that I have learned is that I do not need to have the answer. Perhaps you are thinking, "Well, of course you don't, God is answering through you." Yes, that is true, but that is only the beginning. Through my exploration, I learned that I connected my worthiness to my ability to 'perform', which included solving things for others. I began to connect my ability to help others, listen, provide for them, and create solutions as the definition of worthiness. It created a constant striving and cycle of doing to satisfy my own sense of worth. It kept me in a constant state of sacrificing myself. As you might imagine, I created a cycle of exhaustion as I tried to keep up with being that version of myself across most of the relationships in my life.

I remember a leadership session where the coach said, "Don't be the go-to person, they never get promoted." As she described the plight of the "go-to" person, I remember feeling awe-struck. There was an ah-ha moment about how I positioned myself at work, but that was minimal in comparison to the insight I had in that moment. I began seeing how I would always feel this level of martyrdom if I continued to try to have all the answers and to be whatever the situation or person needed from me in the moment. I was contorting myself over and over to satisfy my desire to 'achieve' so I could feel that I had earned my worthiness. That cycle lasted decades, beginning in childhood and continuing at the time I began writing this book.

Worth is a personal definition and is deeply connected to your relationship with the divine. It is my clear desire for people to know the truth about worthiness. You are worthy. God requires nothing from you, as it was Their initial declaration that defined you as worthy. Remember that God sees all and knows all. They witness you fully, including your thoughts, and still call you worthy. This is an invitation to accept Their definition as your own. You are worthy. That's all. No disclaimers, qualifications, or addenda. There is no earning worthiness; it is inherent. Sometimes people will indeed want others to "prove" their worth, but that is an ego-centered request. It is not the divine truth, and it does not have to be the way you believe that worthiness is established.

At the heart of this revelation is the truth about how we can center others and value their perspectives over our own. Hopefully, you recognize that the power of choice is in your hands. It is not about what others desire to be true. They can't make you prove your worth against a standard that they establish. Only you can decide if performing to their standard is aligned with the way you want to live your life. In my experience, performing for others was still a pathway to rejection, disappointment, or a perpetual void left even when I exceeded their expectations or a stated agreement. What I received in acknowledgment did not fill me up in the ways that I desired. Instead, it kept me striving with mounting resentment. The recognition of resentment was surprising. In so many cases, people hadn't asked me to do what I did; they simply received what I offered. In some cases, what they asked for was minimal in comparison to what I delivered. Eventually, I realized that my resentment or disappointment was not about the current moment but instead had been mounting for years as a reflection of my contorting myself to perform for others. It was simply exhausting. I also recognized that there were people who were comfortable taking as much as I would offer. I was a prime mark for being taken advantage of because I had very few hard boundaries, and I would often bend because I wanted to support others. Others often hurt me, and many of the experiences in my adulthood touched the wounds from my childhood. I would have a journey to forgive myself and others while reconciling the importance of my vulnerability.

Interestingly, I have always known I had a profound capacity to forgive, but I did not want to show it right away. I wanted people to see the impact or hurt they caused. It was a part of the martyr wound within me that needed healing. This means I can forgive and let go. God will work with the person to reconcile their actions and choices just as God works with me on mine. This is still an ongoing body of work for me.

The other big learning for me was this: The experience was nothing like what I thought God would show me. In a relatively recent learning of who I was to God and my role on the earth, the call to connect more deeply with my heart felt like a failure. I went to God that day, ready to hand in my wings. I had already decided I couldn't be who God said I was. In the seconds following my call with my mentor, I had forgotten that God sent her to me with a message to encourage me to keep doing the work to connect with my heart. I was already working on it. I was healing. There was an opportunity to embrace the revelation with optimism that God had given me the capacity to do what was needed. Instead, I reverted to an old pattern of saying, "I'll never be enough." With my metaphorical tail between my legs, I went to God, feeling like a failure. God met me with grace and love. I was reminded of how deeply I matter to God and how vital my gift is. God reminded me that people were waiting for the experience of love and healing that flowed through me. God reminded me that other leaders need the experience God was taking me through and that I was set apart to teach them how to do it. The experience reinforced what it means to have safe and trusted voices that speak for God in a way that is not tainted by our human experience of each other.

All of what I expected this revelation to be was made different the second I sat with God. I felt encouraged to do the hard work that God had before me. It is a space in which I am evolving and will likely continue across the balance of my life. I am so grateful for all of it because it has shown me who I am.

The big lesson is to trust God with your healing. Why would God highlight an area to you that doesn't matter? Why would God ask you to heal something you don't have the capacity to heal? God equips us to heal in ways that reveal truth to us. The more I focus on healing things that come up as God shows me me, the more I love the me that God designed.

Clearing Energy Blocks

With an understanding of energy and the fact that it is meant to move constantly, it is reasonable to ask how to address energy blocks. Movement, addressed in the previous section, is one of the most effective ways to clear blocks. It is true that simply moving your body will help you clear stagnant energy. There are lots of other ways to clear blocks as well. One of the best ways to remove blocks is to bring your attention to your breath. Breathwork can be done anywhere, and there are multiple ways to engage in the practice. It can be used to help you create a deep focus. Some practices will help you raise your energy level and give yourself a burst to take on the challenges ahead. You can utilize the practice to release stress and anxiety. It is also helpful in preparing for sleep. Meditation and breathwork practices can help you reset the cortisol response in the body when you practice for 20 minutes or longer.

In the inset section, "God Show Me Me," prayer is described as a tool to connect with the divine. Prayer is a powerful way to clear energy, center intentions, and invite in the energy and healing you desire. Prayer can often feel difficult to start for those unfamiliar with it. There are several resources that can help you create a regular system of prayer in your life. Joining a prayer group, finding the right spiritual or religious affiliation, or even convening with a few family members or friends can help create discipline and grow your comfort with prayer. There is one very important thing to know. You can't get it wrong. Really. It's that simple. Pray your heart. Be genuine and pure in your intentions, and you can't get it wrong.

Of course, some systems and frameworks can be useful. Still, nothing will supersede the effectiveness of someone who comes forth genuinely seeking the love of the divine and earnestly wants to worship, receive forgiveness, and desire a relationship. Getting started with prayer is like talking to your best friend. You dial them up and say hello. Your heart does the rest. God knows you better than anyone there ever was in the world.

Prayer helps move energy in ways that are difficult to understand in our humanness. Somehow, in the brilliance of God, the heaviness of hearts is lifted, peace is felt, and the healing of being witnessed is experienced. As you grow more directive in your prayer life, you will explore ways to move energy and create pathways for healing. Start by considering how to incorporate it into your desire to move energy.

Favorite Ways to Clear Energy

As a kid, I loved going to ice cream stores. There was a place up the hill from the South Orange Village called Gruning's Ice Cream.

It was there for over 80 years. I don't remember how many flavors they offered, but I know I never had a bad one. I loved the variety, and clearly, the founders of other ice cream businesses have found the secret. Even though people may have favorites, most desire variety and an opportunity to try something new.

I believe the same applies to the practices we use to reset ourselves. I have friends who clearly know that they need time outside every day. I have a grounding mat so that I can experience grounding whenever I need to, regardless of the weather outside. I can remember the first time I went outside to ground. I was looking around as if I were waiting for something to happen. It was odd to me. Whatever I thought I would feel while I did it, did not happen. Over time, I realized that it was the way I felt afterward that cemented it on my list of ways I recharge. To know me is to see that I have an aversion to putting my feet on the dirt. Sand, no problem. Dirt, no thanks, until I learned the benefits of grounding. My point to you is to explore the options multiple times before deciding that something won't work for you. Your openness to the experience, preconceived notions, and past experiences are influencing factors, so start by exploring your beliefs and feelings about the practices before you begin. You may want to ask some powerful questions:

What is possible for me to experience if I choose to truly be open to the experience?

How might what I experienced in the past be influencing this moment?

I recognize that I am a different person now. How
might this practice support my continued growth?

The point is to be curious and open to the experience. Remember that it is entirely possible to try the right thing at the wrong time. Reflect from a place of curiosity.

My absolute favorite way to clear energy is prayer. I love to talk, and God is my favorite listener. I also pray by listening to God and my own heart, but in essence, it is the art of conversation grounded in goodness and love that releases whatever is weighing me down. Prayer is part of my makeup, and it is my language of love to God and Humanity.

I meditate regularly and do breathwork. Guided imagery is one of my favorite ways to help others clear energy, and I incorporate breathwork into my practice most of the time.

Walking and yoga are my favorite ways to use movement to clear my energy. In more recent times, I have had phenomenal experiences with QiGong.

I enjoy massages and bodywork, which also help to move energy. Painting is another favorite of mine.

Lastly, clearing clutter is something I consider different from cleaning. Some people find cleaning to be a highly effective way to move energy. I find that a specific project focused on decluttering gives me something to focus on, a clear outcome at the end, and joy as I release what I no longer need.

As you think about clearing energy blocks, it may benefit you to consider factors like your environment and the people around you. When considering the environment, consider that energy moves freely in nature. Spending time outside is a great way to clear your mind. The elements are present outside, naturally placing you in a space to give and receive. For example, consider the natural relationship between people and plants. The beautiful cycle of life allows each to purify the air for the other. You can enjoy a natural relationship as you exchange energy through breath. Grounding is another powerful way to move energy. Studies have demonstrated that it is a natural way to heal the body. By placing your bare feet on the ground outside, particularly in grass/dirt, you allow the stagnant energy in your body to move. The Earth's healing energy impacts your body, creating a balance of the energy within us.

Notice how you feel when you walk into a space. Can you feel what is present before people begin speaking to you? What does walking into a space with good energy and feeling welcome feel like? What do you choose when the places you are in have stagnant energy? What active choices are you making? You can decide to change the energy in the space or perhaps leave the space, which is how you shift energy.

As you heal, it will be difficult to ignore how you feel around others. Remember that your choice to heal does not mean they will choose to heal, or that you will move through the journey at the same pace. A good place to start is grounding yourself in the truth that this is your journey and that you choose to move in accordance with your timing. Actively decide to release the healing time of others to what is decided between them and God. It will free you to do the same for yourself. Begin to carve more time for yourself to cultivate practices that help you clear energy rather than respond to the energy that others bring into your space. The more time you have directing your own energy, the more equipped you will feel to keep that same energy as you engage with others.

Choose Joy

Next to love and peace, Joy is what I believe to be the most powerful emotion. Some describe Joy as having the highest vibration, and I believe that to be accurate. In my experience, all three can be present regardless of what else is happening around you. These choices keep you connected to the fabric of who you are. They are your truth. I love talking about joy. It is not fully understood and more infrequently experienced by people. Happiness and joy are often used interchangeably, but they do not mean the same thing. Happiness is a momentary experience. Joy is a state of being. Joy can be experienced despite changes in immediate circumstances. Joy is not given to you; it is not external to you. Another person can create an environment where happiness is a readily available choice. For example, a loved partner creating a beautiful marriage proposal celebration would most likely be an environment where their partner chooses happiness. Joy is the state that the person chooses to experience regardless of whether there is a celebration or a difficult and uncertain time.

Joy is similar to faith. To have joy is to decide, 'despite what I see or feel in the immediate, my knowing assures me that all is well and all will be well'. Joy gives us a powerful tool to counter the old patterns of being overwhelmed by changing circumstances and frozen by fear. Joy reminds you that there is another choice. You can invite fear and other emotions to travel in their proper place.

When you choose joy, you invite a different energy into your life. You begin to experience life through a different lens. A general gratitude marks the awareness of your experience of being alive and aware. The more you choose joy, the more it swells within you. The frame it creates in your life supports you in carrying hope and wonder into the dark corners of life.

To choose joy is to go on a journey. Try journaling about when you have experienced joy. How might you choose joy more intentionally if it is not your ongoing companion? What are you willing to release to invite joy back into your life? Consider that joy, faith, hope, and love are multipliers in your life. When they are present, they grow, multiplying their positive effects. When emotions like fear, worry, anxiety, and overwhelm are present, they reduce the efficacy of emotions like joy. To be clear, all of these emotions are important and welcome in life. They all have a role. It's essential to recognize the significance of each leading influence and its duration. This requires both attention and purpose. By intentionally choosing joy, you can cultivate a positive environment for your healing process.

Shaping Your Mindset for Healing

Healing and mindset go hand in hand. Both impact each other. As you strengthen and shift your mindset, you will find that healing occurs more naturally and with more ease. Healing can happen irrespective of your mindset; however, it is like forcing your way through a locked door. Of course, you can break it down, but you will damage the frame, door, and the surrounding structure. The simplest way is to unlock it. The key is shifting your mindset and grounding yourself in the positive beliefs you desire to shape your world.

How do you address mindset? Remember that "Perspective Changes Everything." One of the most powerful tools we have is reframing current circumstances. Healing starts with a decision to accept what has already occurred. It is impossible to heal something that you cannot begin to accept. Accepting it fully creates more ease in the healing journey. That is the ideal situation. Knowing that you can begin to heal even without full acceptance is wonderful. Let's look at why that happens.

Acceptance is an acknowledgement of an occurrence. It is not the same as agreement or an acquiescence to its occurrence. It is an acknowledgement. Often, the desire is to become okay with a situation, but ask yourself for the truth at this moment. How can you fully agree with something you did not ask for or intentionally create? Agreement is something that can be achieved down the road. For example, after accepting an argument between you and your partner, you can later agree that it was beneficial because each of you learned something about the other. Agreeing that it benefited you somehow is a byproduct of experiencing the healing that begins with acceptance.

Much of acceptance is met with regret when it comes to healing. It is human to lament the things that have happened, whether intentionally or not. As described earlier in the book, many traumas are embedded in our DNA and carried for multiple generations. We cannot always find the apparent root cause for our "Why." If you are someone who needs to know why or pinpoint the starting point for a condition that needs healing in the present, it may be difficult for you to facilitate healing on your own. The why is less important in the immediate term; what matters now is accepting that things happened, so your healing may begin.

Acceptance is a tool that will significantly benefit you beyond the healing work you start at the moment. Learning to embrace life with acceptance, without agreement, will free you to move through life without collecting more circumstances that require healing.

Health

Care of our health or physical self is largely focused on caring for what is visible on the outside or properly diagnosed by a licensed physician. In general, people focus on what can be seen or known. This is often evidenced by treating a symptom without clarity around the underlying condition. A reactionary approach is also par for the course. To heal, proper connections must be made between what is seen and experienced and what is felt and exists below the surface. The physical body connects to all things. The connection between the other parts of self, emotional, mental, and spiritual, must be healthy to truly heal.

You have likely witnessed someone battling with issues around maintaining a healthy weight. Nutrition, specialty diet, and exercise are the most common ways people address weight. With a myopic focus on the physical, drive and commitment typically wane, and results are fleeting. The answer to why is found within the connection to mindset, emotions, and behavior. Commitment waivers when you are unsure whether you can achieve the goal or fear that you will do all that is required and still end up disappointed. The emotional linkage to behaviors is very powerful and often misunderstood. Suppose you are unaware of the underlying fears around failing or perfectionism, which can stand in the way of creating commitments. In that case, you might struggle to understand why the physical efforts are not moving the needle as you desire.

Underneath it all, everything is connected, and how we see ourselves in the physical matters. The root of the conditions we experience
in our physical body is generally traceable to emotions and patterns
of thinking and behavior. Our spiritual self or soul remembers what
is true and its purposeful design. The answers to our physical self are
connected deeply to the soul's journey, yet we are so often disconnected from spirit that we cannot even see the suffering we cause ourselves.

Even though you want to get to the core of the "how" question,
you have to ground yourself in the why. The answers are actually in
your understanding and acceptance of what is happening underneath
the surface. In this case, exploring the connection between the physical
manifestation of conditions within will help you to make a lasting
healing change. That sustained change becomes a part of how you
are in your physical body. This decision to apply mindful approaches,
grant yourself grace when regressing, and boldly explore where behaviors come from marks the real healing journey.

Let's look at some connections to help you further understand the
healing pathways for the body.

Movement

One of the most important things we can do to support overall health
and well-being is to ensure that movement is an ongoing part of life
and the healing journey. Because we are energy, we need movement.
Movement reminds us to reconnect with parts of ourselves. Think
back to a time you sat for a while and then stood up. Your initial
reaction was likely to stretch. These moments of connectivity call us to
be present with the body. Your body was reminding you that it needed

more than just standing. The stretch incorporated more muscles and helped you expand your lungs as you breathed more deeply.

Movement offers us a way to connect with ourselves, see what we need, and remember that we are more than our thoughts. Exercise is one of the regular ways that people think about incorporating movement into their lives. It is a beautiful way to express love and care for our bodies. Often, the practice can be used against the body as a form of punishment. It is important to realize that what might help you create a physical outcome that looks desirable on the outside can cause damage to other parts of the body. In essence, consider using positive reinforcement and encouragement instead of negative self-talk and punishment for choices. The desire to "make yourself pay" for failing to do something, eating something, or other disciplinary-led reasoning is more harmful than you might realize. Choose exercise to honor your body and its capabilities. Think about what you are building with and inside your body. You can push yourself without creating harm. A healing mindset encourages us to look at ourselves with love and kindness.

Yoga, Qi Gong, Pilates, and Tai Chi are practices that center on or incorporate mindfulness. While you can be mindful in any movement, it may help you connect with your body and spirit to add a practice like this into your healing journey. For some, these practices may be overlooked because of their religious origins. The choice to see this as a religious practice is an individual choice. This is one of the many paradigms that need to be healed. The best filter is to sit with God and ask whether or not a movement practice is right for you and is honored by God. Similarly, you can ask your body what it needs. You can still your mind and ask what is needed. It is truly that simple. People choose to make the simple complex. Breathwork and movement have healing properties with incredible health benefits available to you. The value of being able to bring your mind and breath into the present moment is immeasurable.

Dancing is another way to incorporate movement. Dancing gets the body moving, raises your energy, and can become a spiritual and freeing expression of love. It is one of the best ways to shift your mood instantly. Dancing releases endorphins, which help us feel uplifted. There is more to what is possible here. Since movement allows us to release tension in the body and connect with our energy, dancing takes it up to another level. When you dance, it is possible to release pent-up emotions. By allowing the body to free flow, you can tap into the body's energy and release or generate feelings. This is a great way to connect deeply with emotion and release stagnant energy. Dancing needs no tools and can be done without a specific form when you choose to allow yourself to be in flow. Healing is present as you allow yourself to be fully experienced through movement.

More examples of movement are provided in a later chapter of the book. When considering movement, remember that it does not have to be complicated. Incorporating a daily walk is a beautiful way to incorporate movement. Try pairing the walk with a reflection on the day or as a time to set intentions for yourself. Another way to open yourself up to healing is to practice being present. Using a daily walk to be present in the environment is a great way to observe life outside of your interests. Take a stroll in various directions, appreciating nature's beauty and observing social interactions. Pay attention to the emotions that arise as you engage with the world around you. Part of healing is leaning in to feel the longing within that wants to be seen. In this moment, pause to reflect on how movement can honor the parts within you calling out for love.

The Gut

Fortunately for the world, gut health has gained more prominence, and access to support and practitioners has improved. There is still much to be learned, and most importantly, the linkages between behavior and mindset to heal the gut. Gut health is more than pre, probiotics, kombucha, and enzymes. The gut is misunderstood. Many people do not know that the gut is home to a brain for the body. It contains its own nervous system, the enteric nervous system, which is sometimes considered a part of the central nervous system. The emotional receptors in the gut are believed to comprise more than 100 million nerve cells (Johns Hopkins Medicine, "The Brain-Gut Connection). This makes up what is commonly considered to be our second brain. This second brain is responsible for communicating with the brain and is the seat of emotions in our body.

The term "gut feelings" comes from the fact that there are emotional receptors in the gut. The gut operates in conditions that are often less than optimal. Our eating, sleeping patterns, digestion, parasites, and emotions compromise our gut health. This includes emotional distress when we have unresolved trauma and repressive behaviors. This, of course, is an incomplete list. Allow these examples to paint a picture for you.

Imagine the drain of a sink, a traditional system without a garbage disposal, with no strainer. In a household of 4, the system would quickly become clogged if even two of the four are unaware of the impact of rinsing debris down the drain without a strainer. If each of the four is only conscious of what they are allowing into the drain, they would lack the perspective of having multiple people dumping into the drain. First, the system would become sluggish, and eventually, it would become clogged, and then it would fail to work as intended.

This is what happens within our gut. The physical self is digesting what you eat and moving waste through its pathways to exit the body. The emotional self stores emotions and feelings that are not readily processed within our gut. As emotions are ignored, they are stored with repressed emotions, fears, anxiety, and more. Imagine them growing exponentially within the gut, always present and ready to overflow at a moment's notice, as the only way out is to come back up, since the pathway out is sluggish.

Turn your attention to your thoughts. While thoughts live in the brain, the connection between thoughts and gut health is substantiated. There is ongoing research at Johns Hopkins to further understand the impact of "digestive system activity and cognition." According to the article, thinking skills and memory are believed to be impacted. If you think about brain health for a moment, it is substantiated that addictive substances, including sugar, cause conditions in the brain, like "brain fog." If the ingestion of refined sugars could cause "brain fog," imagine the impact of the sugar sitting in the gut at different stages of digestion and through the intestinal tract as waste. In the same way, the lack of clarity can impact our thinking and sensing, and part of the related thought process is impacted, meaning the connection from the gut to the brain.

As you reflect on how gut health is impacted by what we eat, movement, how we process emotions, and the linkage to our thoughts, you can begin to see your own patterns and why healing is important. Remember the sink analogy. Here, we have outlined three of the four family members and a few ways they can clog the drain, i.e., impact the gut. But what about your spiritual self? The fourth area is equally important.

The gut is the home of our intuitiveness. Things like faith are felt and then become a more concrete thought. Our knowing and even the way those who believe in the holy spirit experience the feeling in the gut before accepting that feeling as a thought in the brain. The divine communicates through the heart. The heart-gut connection is, in essence, emotionally centered. Spirit is an emotional connection within, so anything that blocks the movement of energy within will impact our connectedness. We can still achieve connection, but the strength of the connection is enhanced by freeing our minds and hearts. Connecting to our divinity is simply easier when we are less encumbered in our mind and body.

More and more studies, practitioners, and modalities are emerging to help you care for your gut. Gut health is a perfect example of how your healing team can support you. Each of your healing team members has some connection to your gut! Your therapist, physician, nutritionist, and spiritual coach are all interested in the health of your gut. It matters to the effectiveness of each specialty's roles in your overall health. Gut healing is a journey.

To begin, observe your relationship with your gut. How do you feel about your gut? Are you protective of it? Do you hold things in? Do you ignore your gut instincts or dismiss them as unimportant? Merely drawing your attention to your gut is a starting point. Be curious. What can you observe that will help you determine how to love your gut more?

Managing your emotions is an important step. Even if you are not ready to address the stored emotions, being aware of how you work through current emotions in a healthy way will help. You will become more conscientious and will begin a pattern of handling emotions in the moment. The shift will help you become more confident in feeling your emotions and releasing them in ways that benefit your overall health.

Another place to focus is on nutrition and a healthy diet. What are you putting into the theoretical drain? What steps can you take to put more fresh and nutritious food into your body? What nutrients are you missing in your current diet? How can you incorporate foods that help your body heal? Exercise and other practices that address physical conditions are helpful as well. Many modalities can address gut health. Acupuncture, acupressure, chiropractic, massage therapy, and stretch labs are excellent ways to support your gut health improvements. Yoga offers beautiful mind-body connections during poses that target your gut and midsection. You get the picture. There are lots of options. Start by becoming more aware and then identifying a course of action with your team.

While resources are discussed later in the book, it is important to focus on the greatest resource for your healing: YOU. Do your best to appreciate the importance of your knowledge of yourself. Quiet your mind. What is your gut telling you that it needs? Allow yourself to listen without judgement. This is not about what you ate or the last time you exercised. Strengthening this connection is an act of self-love. It is a promise to get progressively better at listening and honoring yourself. It is a choice to allow your truth, voice, and soul to unite once again on your journey to become who you are called to be. This promises to be more powerful than you can see or imagine at this moment. Who would have guessed that so much of who you are is locked within your gut? The blessing is that you hold the key, and time is on your side.

Skin

As the largest organ in the body, the skin significantly impacts our health more than we may recognize. Our skin protects our organs and systems in the body. It is a filter, a purification system, with pathways for toxins to leave the body. Skin helps us regulate the temperature of the body and experience sensations. It is equally absorbent, taking in elements from the air and any substances applied directly to it. Awareness of the external environment and recognition of potential toxins are a part of conscious skincare. Your skin breathes, eats, and sheds. It is alive.

Keeping the skin breathing is important for our overall health. Caring for the skin includes removing the dead skin cells that collect on the outer layer of the dermis. Intentional removal of the excess skin cells helps to ensure the skin's overall health. Dry skin brushing is a common practice that has multiple benefits. In addition to exfoliation, it can stimulate the lymphatic system when done correctly. Keeping the lymphatic system flowing is critical for overall health.

Consider the skin's absorption ability, temperature regulation, and its protective function. It might help to think of the role that the roof of a house plays. It is the first layer of protection when rain comes. It shields the structure below from the rain and pushes the rain away from the home through the drainage systems. Gutters, for example, will ensure that the water is projected away from the house to protect the foundation. If the gutters are clogged, the rainwater will find any other available pathways to drain. If the roof has damage, leaks will begin. Blocked gutters can also cause a buildup, leading to leaks that compromise the roof's stability.

Skin is similar. Your skin is both the roof and the gutters. What you choose to put on and expose your skin to should be carefully considered. There is a beautiful life lesson that we can derive from the skin. When we are thoughtful about how we treat our bodies on the inside, the skin becomes more purified. In many cultures today, the focus and attention are on the outside of the body. Often, this means making cosmetic adjustments and using unhealthy chemicals that clog up the skin and lock the toxins inside, looking for another way to move out of the body. The toxins and waste within the body need a pathway out. They do not belong inside and threaten the body's foundation, just like the clogged gutters in a home.

The most important realization here is this: The body was created as a system of perfection. It can cleanse, heal, and grow all on its own. It was created to do what is needed to care for itself. As long as you, the caretaker of the body, take care of it, it will have the right conditions it needs to be healthy. Our skin often shows us when there is something wrong inside the body. You could liken it to the rain pouring over the side of the gutters rather than flowing through the drain properly. Immediately, you know that something is clogged; it is a signal that action needs to be taken. When we cover up our skin and hide the conditions from ourselves, we ignore the signal that something must be addressed.

As a lifetime sufferer of eczema, I know what that is like. As a child, I can remember being itchy all the time. I would observe new eczema patches popping up in new places, each more uncomfortable than the next. Most were in clothed parts of my body in my youth, but by the time I was in high school, I had patches on my eyelids and my neck. One of my favorite teachers in high school also had eczema. I remember the patches on the back of her hands and recognized the raised skin and small patches where it had been scratched to reveal the flesh below. I identified with it. I had scratched patches of eczema on my inner thigh until it bled.

I had terrible itchy nights, scratching myself in my sleep uncontrollably. It was isolating and embarrassing. I remember being afraid to go to sleep at a sleepover because I was afraid my friends would think something was wrong with me because I was so itchy. I didn't want to fall asleep before them. I was clean. I showered daily. I used creams and lotions to moisturize the area and fight the inflammation. But I still felt the stigma of something being "wrong." I did not know the root cause of my condition, but I knew that it made me feel ugly, uncomfortable, embarrassed, and marked. Marked. As if I had done something wrong to "get" eczema and not know how to heal it. If you had told me back then that my body had the answer to healing it, I would not have believed you. It didn't seem like anything could help.

In my adulthood, I continued to struggle with it, although it became better as I became more consistent with applying medicated creams. I remember learning that using hydrocortisone creams and other treatments made being in the sun risky for my skin in those areas. I was not happy about that. I loved the sun. My dermatologist directed me to reduce the temperature of my shower to tepid. That was like asking me to do the cold plunge (more to come in a later chapter). I absolutely froze at the idea of cold water on my skin, even on the hot and humid summer days. The only cold water I could tolerate was the ocean, simply because being in the water was heaven for me, regardless of the temperature. The other issue is that a hot shower was the equivalent of a cup of coffee in the morning.

In the same way that some people cannot function without their morning caffeine, I needed my super hot shower to feel truly alive. So you can imagine that the thought of a tepid shower was one that I could not say yes to doing daily. I reduced the temperature slightly, but I have never stuck to a daily tepid shower. I did understand the reasoning, but I also recognized that it was a way to improve external conditions, not heal the root of my eczema.

In my adulthood, I began to learn more about my condition and release the shame I felt connected to it. I became more open to discussing it, leading to people sharing resources and their learnings with me. I can remember sharing a book I read with a friend whose son played basketball with my son. She shared the book and pieces of my story with someone she loved, who was able to find some solutions that helped him experience more progress on his healing journey. That book, "The Eczema Detox," lives on my bookshelf and holds a wealth of knowledge. I want to be transparent that I did not follow all of the recommended regimens in the book. As with anything, including this book, your work is to explore, listen, and connect with your body to learn the right path for you. I found so many confirming things in the book; more than anything, I was convinced that my body had been speaking to me all along. I became emboldened to listen to it, and my eczema began to heal.

It will not surprise you to learn that the beginning of my eczema was rooted in my gut. Sure, there are hereditary factors, but there were other things. I ate a ton of sugar as a kid, a ton. When I was in middle school, my mom changed our diet significantly. She removed sugary cereals, soda, and candy and began on a path to more conscious eating. We eventually eliminated all meats beyond poultry, fish, and seafood. I had stopped drinking milk years before, after an incident with sour milk. From that moment forward, my body entirely rejected drinking milk, although I occasionally ate ice cream and enjoyed a milkshake on a rare occasion.

So, let's look at what this means. My body began to reject cow's milk in its pure form. Something within my body said, "This isn't for us anymore," but I continued to find other ways to ingest it. My body didn't protest the ice cream, milkshakes, and milk-based desserts that I ate in the way it would have if I attempted to drink a glass of milk, but instead, it reacted in another way. That's right. My eczema would pop up. Angry red skin with a scaly white covering- bumpy and itchy. It would call out to me, asking for answers as to why I would keep this cycle going, but I wasn't listening. I wasn't aware that this was how my body wanted to communicate.

Later in my adulthood, I began to listen. I started working on my gut health to eliminate my lifetime constipation issues. That journey led me to understand that I needed to love my body and be willing to release things. As I began seeking answers from my body, I started to notice the impact of trigger foods. Aged cheese, for example, will cause an almost immediate reaction. There were specific spots where the rash would emerge in response. I began to note the differences in the rash. What did it mean when it was dry and ashy? When it was red and raised? How long did they last? Was what I ate, my elimination, my stress level, or other factors that triggered or contributed to the environment? I became a student of my body.

A few years ago, I was bold enough to dare God to heal my eczema. For those who feel taken aback by the word "dare," please find yourself in good company. It felt bold, brazen maybe, to dare God. My thinking was this. "God, I know you can do all things. I believe you can. I still have this eczema, although I have been listening to my body, addressing my diet, and paying more attention to my skin. I know you have the answers, so I dare you to heal it as a testimony to what you can do." It was bold. I shared it publicly, and guess what? God did it. I went months without a flare-up. I was so grateful. I shared the testimony, although I feared I might somehow mess it up. And one day, the eczema popped back up. It came in the place I call "the mother." It's the spot I have identified as the core of my condition. When that heals fully, I will know that my eczema will be permanently gone.

So, of course, I went back to God to ask why. God showed me what They could do. It was now time for me to do my part. God began to reveal the conditions within my body. They showed me what needed to change for me to fully heal the root cause of all my issues. In the best way I can describe it, I am healing levels and layers of my life. As I heal old traumas and patterns, they have triggered spots in my eczema that connect back to times in childhood when those specific spots were active.

Imagine for a moment seeing yourself as a baby. Envision a beautiful pearlescent bubble encapsulating you. Imagine another bubble forming around you on your second birthday and so forth. Like looking at the layers of a croissant, in adulthood, you also have many layers around you. When we heal, we start at the outermost layer. Even though you may want to target something specific, you have to be able to move through the outer layers to get to that healing. When you are healing many things at one time (as opposed to targeted healing), you heal layer by layer. This allows things to emerge and be exposed as you are ready to address them.

My healing now is not simply about my eczema. It is about my full self. It is healing my emotions, releasing repression, and helping me accept myself, while also being centered in my truth. Many different things have emerged as each layer is addressed and the underlying conditions and environment are healed. It might not come as a shock to hear that anxiety and fear have been central to my struggles. These emotions have significantly contributed to my digestive issues, making me more susceptible to various triggers for dis-ease, including certain foods. To fully benefit from the healing I believe God has already provided, I need to make choices that align with this understanding. This involves viewing my body as a vessel for God's work, which means treating it with greater care—both in terms of what I consume and what I apply to it.

One of the commitments that I have made to care for my skin is to put on it things that are edible. As I read the labels of the products I use, I ask myself whether or not I would consume them orally. Of course, that may not work for someone who has not chosen to reduce or avoid chemically enhanced and modified foods, but if you are more conscientious about what you eat, you may find this practice to be helpful. Try asking yourself if you know what each ingredient is and then whether or not you feel comfortable eating it. The practice has helped me become more aware of what is out there and what matters to my skin, and most importantly, I have actively assumed the role of COO of my health. God will provide the healing, but whether or not I experience it is contingent on my working in alignment with the plan for better health. My CEO's blueprint is good. I have to put it into operation and manage it on an ongoing basis. We will have what we expect. I expect to heal it fully and hold myself accountable to better care for my body day after day.

Acceptance and Perspective in Healing

Earlier in this chapter, we explored how shaping your mindset begins with creating space for new beliefs and possibilities. Now, let's look at another critical aspect, how acceptance and perspective shifts can open the way for deeper, more sustainable healing. Acceptance is one of the most powerful mindset tools we have. It's not about agreeing with what happened, but acknowledging it fully so that healing can take root. When we approach our thoughts and experiences through this lens, we create a mental environment where change is not forced, but invited.

Yes. Sit with that for a moment. Acceptance is far more difficult when the mind is working in a cluttered, polluted environment. If you are regularly practicing meditation or another form of mindfulness, you are ahead of the crowd. For most, though, this mental noise is the default. Learning to accept what has happened, and to reframe it, becomes a way of clearing space not just for calm, but for the deeper shifts that healing requires.

Imagine you are piloting a plane, and it is time to land. You are approaching the runway, only to find the runway is crowded with planes, fuel tankers, repair crews, and vehicles everywhere you look. How could you possibly land the plane? Not only is there the absence of a clear landing strip, but there is not enough runway to land, and there is much less space to taxi to the gate. If your objective is to complete the flight safely and arrive at the gate without incident, it is simply impossible to believe you will achieve it. This is equivalent to what we attempt to do daily.

We wake up with our minds relatively open, and before starting the day, many are digesting the fear-laced opinions of others through news, social media, and even conversations with our partners and family. Somehow, holding space for others has become the most important thing we do each day. It's no wonder that the runway becomes congested.

Your mindset will reflect what you believe, digest, observe, fear, and embrace. It is a great filter in your body. It creates the frame of reference for how you take in and release information to the world. Healing the mind begins with a practice of release.

Let's pause for a moment. Many choose to seek out wisdom or find a new way to do something as the starting point for adjusting their mindset. For example, if someone recognizes a gap in a skill set they desire, the first step is to identify an expert and then buy into their philosophy. It is reasonable, right? Of course. But let's look at what happens over time. That same individual becomes an expert in looking outside for how others have solved their gap. It works for them in most cases because they have actively surrendered their former beliefs. Quite frankly, their expertise could be the very thing that you need to gain the skill you want, but until you adjust your mindset and correlate your beliefs, you will only be able to absorb it at the surface level.

In order to make a genuine change, one has to understand what is out of alignment and be willing to explore their why. Society encourages us to take action to add new beliefs and knowledge without adequately identifying what is in the way. If you agree that landing the plane on a congested runway is not the best way, why try to add methods and modules atop a congested mind?

This is not to suggest that you have to have it all figured out, but you owe it to yourself to release limiting beliefs, conflicting desires, and old patterns before fully embracing something new. Let's focus on how you do that.

"Most people are unfamiliar with their beliefs."

Most people are unfamiliar with their beliefs. Over time, beliefs have formed that have become their way of seeing the world. Until something arises that challenges it, they do not even recognize their thoughts. We rarely check with our thoughts to understand how they are shaping our world. The way that we address the situations in our lives feels like it is happenstance, but the truth is that we are using filters that we have not cleaned. Perhaps we have never cleaned them. Our beliefs build upon each other. They constantly evolve as a product of our experiences and how they reinforce the current mindset or require it to change. Left unchecked, we begin to respond and shift in ways inconsistent with what is most desirable for us.

Healing will always begin with awareness. Whether we choose to become aware or others bring about awareness, some event causes us to look at ourselves. We can take from that the notion that bringing our awareness to our mindset intentionally is the way that we can begin to create the desired shifts. You might wonder what the desired shifts might be. It depends on what you want to be evident in your life.

Intentions are incredibly important in any area of life, especially healing. To start, explore the way that you look at life. You might begin by using a construct that helps you explore the growth mindset. It is not the only way to explore your appetite for risk, change, and possibilities, but it creates a relatively simple language to use as a starting point. You should acknowledge that there is more to be considered than fixed and growth mindsets. We should also consider that because healing is a process, some combination of both mindsets might be exactly what a person needs at this stage in their healing journey or life. In general, be careful of absolutes. In general, absolutes create the very limitations that we are trying to move beyond.

Begin by determining what you want to explore about your mindset. Intention setting might include exploration and desired outcomes. For example, you might decide to explore your appetite for taking risks in relationships or with your career. Many will recommend that you have a firm picture of the future you desire or your future self. That can create a compelling way to craft your path for the future.

The danger lies in limiting our future potential to what we can imagine right now. Your future self is expansive and full of possibilities. You possess countless insights about yourself that you may have forgotten over the years. Perhaps one or 20 of them are important clues to who you are to be in life. Some of these insights could reveal your true purpose in life. As these clues surface, it's important to allow space for all the potential versions of who you can become without dismissing any possibilities prematurely.

You might consider setting intentions for today based on who you are growing towards being. This creates space for you to continuously refine the vision and let go of constraints. For example, you might set an intention to become more comfortable seeking out risks that help you expand your heart. As you build around that intention, you can bring in more components, like how you show up in relationships, what you desire to give, and the kind of emotions you want to headline your journey.

Another area of mindset is pressure testing your current beliefs while bringing your attention to the connected emotions. Often, we may experience a moment when something within us tells us we cannot do something. You can acknowledge the thought and ask where that comes from. "What proof do we have that I would be unsuccessful with this choice?" You should expect that something will surface; after all, your mind does its job really well. Your observation should be focused on the validity of the current situation. What proof can you offer yourself that you would be successful? Do you even require proof? Flexing the mind's current boundaries is vital to healing your mindset. Push against the ease of following the path the mind offers you until you create patterns that support your expansiveness.

Lastly, explore what is shaping your mind. It is important to filter what you take in because it shapes your perspectives and impacts your overall mindset. Are you drawn to negative stories or anecdotes? What is your relationship with others as you listen to the socio-political positioning in the media? What is the language around you from family, friends, and co-workers? Words carry energy and intention. Emotions can be felt when there are no corresponding words. There is a compounding effect in energy when you are in camaraderie with others. It works equally with positive and negative energy.

Let's look at a couple of examples. Take a group of women who pray together weekly. One person enters the group after having an incredibly grueling week, both mentally and physically. They are experiencing a swirl of negative feedback at work and are fairly certain that things are not as solid as they appear at home. She enters the group and takes the risk to share her story. The group rallies around her. They validate her feelings, meet her with empathy, and begin to cover her with prayer. As they pray together, her mood shifts. Their ability to shift the energy of the space clears the heaviness of her mind.

While they did not solve any of the challenges that she faced, they created an environment where she could choose hope. Their stories reminded her of what is possible. It required an active choice on her part to be open to possibilities and required that they would be open to supporting her by sharing themselves. Imagine the uplift in her mindset. When you surround yourself with others who have shared beliefs or who have a possibility mindset, you will find it much easier to believe in what is possible. You will also expand your current mindset to encompass broader possibilities, allowing you to evolve your own beliefs.

The heaviness of negativity can be stirred up within all of us as well. Imagine a small group of entrepreneurs seeking funding for their businesses. They meet regularly to share resources and experiences and support each other by reviewing each other's submissions. After a few difficult rounds of rejections, they attend their regular meeting. One entrepreneur has received good feedback but no funding confirmation letters yet. The balance of the group has not received any funding or encouraging correspondence. One group member has received several rejections since their last meeting.

As they enter the meeting, the group's energy is pretty heavy. The group member with the more positive experience withholds their update after noticing the general experience of the group. They believe that since there is no official "good news," there is no benefit in sharing. They feel that it would not offer any uplift to the group. The member with multiple rejections begins to express their frustration and disappointment. They continuously say they do not want to bring the group down, but continue to speak about the experience with overt negativity. They convey feelings of victimization and lack of control. Their energy depletes the group as they question whether their process is even working. The heaviness of negativity permeates the group, and the person with the encouraging news never shares their light energy.

Intention is an essential factor in both examples. The initial question is whether or not there is an intention. In the second example, there may or may not have been an intention set by the person sharing their reaction to rejection. It is important to note that not setting a clear intention is a decision to operate without intention. It is a decision. While the outcome may be haphazard, there was a decision to allow anything to happen. Often, when people feel overwhelmed by their emotions and desire to be seen, they revert to a child-like release of responsibility for their emotions. As emotional stimuli arise, people respond to them at the level of their healing maturity. In their desire to be seen and to feel better, they let go. Their choice allowed their energy to impact the group.

Given the current mood, the entrepreneur, who had good news to share, decided not to tell the others. Often, we see holding back our light as considerate to others who may not be having a similar experience, but forget that the light of one can bring hope to others. Regardless of why they chose what they did, it is evident that the group made decisions based on their beliefs. No one challenged the group to think positively, even though the group's entire purpose was to encourage and uplift one another. The negative energy was compounded, and it stifled the interest in sharing positive news with the group.

Designing Your Healing Team

As you explore ways to start your healing journey, you may want to capture some of the roles you want to fill on your healing team. Exploring your areas of greatest interest will be helpful before you assemble a team. Explore the areas that have piqued your interest. Read books, follow practitioners, take classes, and talk to your friends and family about what they like to do. This will give you the opportunity to create a community around parts of your healing experiences. In the immediate term, ensure that as you engage in the work, you find the right licensed practitioners or experts to support you. You should always engage a primary care doctor when starting a new health care regimen. A therapist is another critical team member because healing will reveal things you may not be prepared to work through on your own. Integration coaches are another resource that can help you identify what you might need on the healing journey. Select the other members based on the expertise you need for that part of your healing journey. Plenty of resources are available, and The Healing Crusade is a great place to do your healing work individually and with the support of a community.

Chapter Pearls

- Healing is a process with many stages. Give yourself time to explore and try out various modalities, practices, and perhaps new disciplines as you find things that are beneficial to you.

- Exploration of ways to move and clear energy is vital for your healing journey.

- Choosing Joy is a powerful way to shift your perspective.

Journal Prompts

- In what ways has your perspective around your healing journey evolved?

- What is one thing you decided to explore as a result of the recommendations in this chapter?

- Who are some of the people/roles that you want to fill on your healing team? In what ways might a community like The Healing Crusade offer support for your specific journey

Chapter Six

We Are One Soul- The Central Soul

H umanity shares one soul. As a collective, there is a central shared soul that connects all people to each other. The make-up of each person is their individual soul, which includes the finger-print of their previous souls and the fingerprint of the central soul. As an individual, you are connected directly to the Divine, the central soul, your ancestry, and your soul's journey(s). The depth of connec-tion between people is at the heart of the question, "Why heal?" In-dividuals cannot heal fully without shifting the imprint of the central soul. Incremental steps on the healing journey have a profound impact as well. Creating healing within the central soul is a beautiful outcome of one's healing journey. The healing of the individual radiates to the central soul and is accessible to all people.

Most people do not access the central soul or look beyond them-selves to see the impact of their healing. From an unhealed state, people look for someone outside of themselves that they can make responsible. They look to share the responsibility for the undesirable things that exist; these are the things that result in unhealed conditions. Man will generally look for someone or something to share the accountability with. There is always a question beyond the full responsibility of the individual. "Where did this start?" "Why is this something that I have encountered?" "Are others experiencing this, and what do we have in common?" Those questions and the ones like them are indeed valid. Nothing that happens on the earth impacts only one person in one unique moment.

Every time we focus our intentions on healing, we begin casting positive energy for ourselves and the collective. The act of setting the intention opens the way for healing to begin. It is equivalent to opening a doorway. Even if the door is cracked open, energy can flow out and in. The opening is broader than just for one person. Try to envision intention as hope. Hope is contagious; the thought catches fire as people share their hope in possibilities. The intentions we set for healing open the door for healing for yourself and others.

One person looking to heal the generational impact of childhood abandonment opens the doorway for others to experience residual healing. Residual healing is what reaches the central soul. This means that when groups of people choose to heal a similar wound, there can be a massive impact on the wound that exists in the central soul.

The central soul is complex. At the same time that there is healing, additional wounds may be generated as others continue to experience feelings that result in pain, like abandonment, for example. That is why healing the central soul takes collective energy. The good news is that it can be healed with more people focused on their healing and committing to eradicate the behaviors and choices leading to that condition. Healing the central soul can be enhanced by individuals' decisions not to react to the stimulus in the way that they have in the past. Let's consider an example.

Imagine that a family has suffered from verbal abuse across generations. For several generations, there has been a parental figure in the home who is verbally abusive. They are acting through learned behavior as a result of the wounds they suffered as children. In the household today, there are two parents and two children. One parent is not verbally abusive, but to avoid conflict, they are silent when the abuse takes place. Both children suffer from self-esteem issues and are unable to speak their truth. Over time, they determine they are not worthy of their voice, so they do not speak up for themselves. As they grow up, they choose partners that are similar to their experience—verbally abusive or conflict-averse. One of the children chose a partner who is verbally abusive. As they work through their healing, they begin to address the abuse and take risks to speak their truth. Rather than accept the conditions, they choose to leave the relationship to protect their joy and love. They choose to grow rather than shrink. They practice forgiveness and acceptance of themselves and their partner despite the abuse they suffered during the relationship.

The changes in the way they respond to the abuse and the ownership that they take of their feelings and decisions are part of the healing process. Acceptance and choice are a path to freedom. Their decisions are a part of the healing process that impacts the central soul and radiates through the collective. The abused wound receives healing. Imagine each healing step as a jolt of love transmuting the wound in the central soul. Anyone can heal beyond themselves and with pure intentions. They can touch the central soul and inspire profound transformation.

What does it mean to heal beyond themselves? Each time we experience healing, we impact the people around us. Our changes in behavior impact others through our interactions. The potential for healing for others as a result of our changed behavior is present. As people in the family, workplace, or social circles experience differences in an individual, it may influence their healing. When the healing impact touches the family, there is an opportunity for the healing to address wounds in their family lineage.

One way to visualize the impact is to think about the neuropathways in the brain. A signal starts in one part and travels across the tract, impacting the axons along the way. Healing is similar. An individual's healing impact can touch family members directly, impact the lineage, and have the potential to heal the central soul.

The connectivity of the collective makes a case for its importance once again. Envision an entire family unit aligned to heal alcoholism within their family lineage. Their decision helps to heal the lineage from the damage of alcoholism. In their journey, they unpack the root cause of the addiction. The root cause is then addressed through their healing efforts. Addressing root causes is at the core of broadening the residual impact of healing. Navigating through the depth of causation deepens the impact of healing in the lineage and within the central soul.

How can we be certain of a central soul? There is substantial evidence demonstrating the interconnectedness of people. In fact, this has been supported by decades of research and studies. People have studied the connection between people and social conditions, global health crises like COVID-19, climate change, deforestation, and social media, among many other phenomena. According to Maslow's Hierarchy of Needs, belonging is a part of the third level of the journey to self-actualization after satisfying the foundational physiological needs and safety. It is interesting to note that the impacts of the physiological and safety levels can be significantly impacted by the behaviors of other people, particularly when there is no genuine consideration for the effects of one's behaviors on another.

If we simply consider connectivity a byproduct of love and relationships, we miss the conscientious behavior of making considerate footprints on the earth. This means that what each of us chooses to do directly impacts others. Let's consider a few examples of how people have a collective impact.

Poultry Production in the United States

Hall County, located in north Georgia, is home to what is known as the poultry capital of the world. This area, north of the capital city of Atlanta, boasts many meat processing facilities. During the height of the pandemic, Hall County found itself with a massive outbreak of COVID-19. The concentration of cases from March to September reached 7000 reported cases. According to the article, the infection rate was "roughly 40% higher than the rates for the five counties that make up the Atlanta metropolitan area." That is significant given that city centers and urban areas typically had higher incidence rates. This is likely attributed to the proximity of residents to each other, such as apartment living and public transportation, compared to people who live in more rural areas, like most of Hall County.

Interestingly, Georgia's early outbreaks in the spring of 2000 impacted counties with significant poultry production facilities. An executive order signed by the sitting president of the United States precluded meat plants from shutting down due to health concerns. This requirement, likely intended to ensure that the food supply was protected, likely exacerbated the health conditions in the local communities. The work environments, irrespective of safety precautions, require workers to interact in close proximity. In the early stages of the pandemic, "there was no masking, no physical distancing and no plastic dividers at many poultry processors..." Mask utilization may have been optional at times during the height of the pandemic.

Many other factors make this an interesting case study. (It is worth the read). What is most important for our needs is understanding the complexity of decisions and why the awareness of the central soul is so important. Some argue that the decision to keep the plants running was political, given the criticality of poultry to the state's economy. Others might cite the desire to satisfy the safety needs, even though health needs might be compromised. This is one illustration of the multilayered risks facing people during the pandemic. Choices impacted much more than the desire for belonging and love. Indeed, a choice to be a part of a staged walkout or to quit their job would have affected the feelings of belonging and love, but it is much more than that. Ultimately, people were faced with making multilayered decisions where their health, safety, security, and other factors were at risk, and any choice they made had the potential for a widespread impact. The question of whether a worker should go to work, contract the disease, and then spread it to their family or community is highly charged. If that same worker decided to work in a way that aligned with their value of safety, which was misaligned with the company, they would risk job loss, impacting their security. A third option of quitting to protect their health would have financial impacts, and given their personal conditions, many other potential risks, including sacrificing love and belonging. Ultimately, we can see that the interconnectedness of people is evident and incredibly complex.

COVID-19 was not simply a pandemic, although it fully satisfies the formal definition. The economic and social impact reached epic proportions. If we consider the social impact alone, countries experienced significant economic shifts, psycho-social impacts, public policy, and the need for new laws and healthcare needs. The decisions of the individual were scrutinized as vaccination decisions were made. In some countries, vaccination was required. Proof of vaccination became a requirement for travel to many countries to protect their citizens and economy. In social circles, neighbors and families experienced divides over vaccination decisions. The complex decisions around whether or not to vaccinate opened the doors to judgment for many people. Regardless of whether a group decided to vaccinate or not, there was a level of ostracization for those who chose the opposite action.

The interconnectivity of people and their decisions was on full display. Looking further, we can see that the risks were not simply at the level of love and belonging in Maslow's Hierarchy. The risks to the physiological level were impacted by people. Consider the impact of the supply chain during the pandemic. Differing choices of public health policies impacted import and export. There were food shortages and access issues. Decisions about health guidelines varied by country, so the preparation and production of food were at risk. Many food production plants faced shutdowns amidst a high occurrence of positive COVID-19 diagnoses. While there are many factors to consider, it is safe to identify choices around vaccination, social behavior (living conditions, quarantining, etc.), and work environment as contributors to the spread of COVID-19 in those working populations.

What was witnessed as a result were impacts to Maslow's defined safety needs (health, emotional security, financial security, and personal security) and risks to their physiological needs (air, water, food). The pandemic impacted all of these foundational levels of the hierarchy through people's behavioral choices. Our role in reviewing this example is not about identifying a "right or wrong" in the choices made as the world navigated the pandemic. Instead, there is an opportunity to gain a deeper understanding of the impact of individual choices on the collective. If one acts as if their decisions are entirely unilateral, having no potential impact on the lives of others, the collective will suffer. Our central soul calls out for more conscientious decision-making. The group dynamics evident here are significant proof that decisions impact the soul of who we are.

Research on belonging, organizational behavior, group dynamics, and other collective experience work helps us understand connection and impact. Representation studies provide recent examples of the effects when media, businesses, and other mediums are not diverse. The lack of diversity has an adverse effect on individuals in the minority of represented groups. The emotional, mental, physical, and spiritual impact undercuts the potential for humanity to thrive. Ideas are lost while innovation and creativity are stymied. Customers are not served at optimum levels. Communities experience imbalance. Thriving in only one part of the collective will always result in a pull from the other part of the collective. The force to counter the pull takes twice as much effort as it would for the entire society to thrive together.

Connectivity between people is one of the most controversial issues in the world today. At our core, we long to be accepted, belong, and be loved. We have the foundational responsibility to create that for ourselves, including the origin of all connections, the Divine. Innately, we understand that beyond ourselves, we have to impact other people to exist in the world.

Even those who choose a reclusive lifestyle will find that they need others for things like sourcing food and access to gasoline or other energy sources. Even with the technology we use, there are people responsible for building, maintaining, and making decisions about the process, even if at a minimal level. The connection may not be directly to another human, but interdependency exists.

In the world today, there is a growing distance between people. There is a visible difference that has grown with the infusion of technology supporting connection through means that do not require a physical connection. Still another kind of distance is presence; the distance that keeps people from connecting through the heart.

There is a growing apathy that replaces empathy. People have chosen to observe as things happen to others, distancing their hearts from the necessity to take action. What is most concerning is that self-centered behavior is now accompanied by righteous indignation or outrage that people with substandard conditions would address their concerns. Instead of the desire to compare their existence to others' plight, a more productive response is to encourage others to address what is inequitable and to support the shift in any way plausible. The response of outrage is telling. It simply says, "You should not have what you believe you should have." If this gives you pause and a feeling of conflict, you should explore it. What makes you believe that each person is not entitled to desire what they believe is a humane, equitable, and abundant existence? Is that not what you desire for yourself? The distance between people has allowed the erosion of consideration for others and a disconnect from their experiences.

Humanity desires to be consistent in its experiences of the world. People constantly look to repeat patterns that enable them to stay in loops of old behaviors. This phenomenon is more than just familiar; it represents the way the brain works to keep people "safe." This cycle enables humans to do things the same way without much thought or focus on whether or not it is serving its ultimate purpose. The desire to continue the familiar cycles works in opposition to the need for change and healing. As one gives into the old cycle, the opportunity to heal that is available at that moment is missed. The more we repeat a behavior that does not serve us, the more deeply embedded that behavior is in how we experience the world.

When we look at the state of affairs worldwide right now, there's a clear division between people. This division is more profound and more complex than it has ever been in the past. Historically, there have been some typical divisors for people that are both expected and somewhat understood, if not accepted. Core examples are religion, gender, race, and social status. In our current climate, how people separate themselves from others is incredibly dynamic. There are sub-groups within the old criteria for separation. In addition to the sub-groups, thought positions now provide another layer of perspectives. Interestingly, people point to the formal elimination of processes of separation, like the historical segregation of the United States, without recognition that an entirely new and more threatening way of being has emerged in its place.

The root emerges from the fact that their hearts are disconnected from each other. It's not simply about creating dividing lines based on features we can see. Instead, it's about all of the ways that people's observed behavior is interpreted. It extends to the assumptions made about whether others are better or less than how we feel they should be. This is symptomatic of inequalities that exist within our heart space.

For example, in the past, a person might have looked at someone else and judged them based on their nationality, race, ethnicity, or age. In the current times, the assessment and subsequent disconnect delve deeper into many of these and other variables.

The type of work a person does is often another factor that people use to create inequality between people. In fact, there are moments when one is looking at all of those elements, as well as political opinions or other social matters. They are assessing and struggling to accept others' opinions about social issues like gun control, the legalization of marijuana, social welfare, and healthcare, as examples. People have moved past disagreement into a state of offense when others do not fully agree with them. The difference in perspective, an excellent tool for learning, turns into grounds for dislike, progressing into hatred, and even to the extreme of wanting to injure others.

Let's look at the legalization of cannabis in the United States as an example. It created quite a stir across the country. Cannabis is a plant with natural properties that adapts to a system in the body, appropriately named as it works with the cannabinoid system inside the physical body of all people. It stands to reason that there could be some medicinal benefit to people because it supports a system that already exists in the body. In the US, it was illegal to grow, sell, and buy it until recently. Utilization and accessibility are still not consistent across the country. It is of interest that while it was considered illegal in the US, the country invested money in international research of Cannabis utilization until there was an opportunity to turn it into a revenue stream for the country. The irony is that many other countries around the world have already legalized the use and purchase of cannabis.

A few issues were at the core of the delay in legalizing it in the US. Interestingly, the root was not the health benefits of the plant. The concern focused on who would earn from the development of the sales and taxation process. The tracking system and integrations provided additional complexity. Another question that loomed before the decision-makers focused on the impact of changing legislation. They had to determine what would happen to those who were found guilty of breaking a law of something that has now been legalized. That created concern about the precedent that would be set.

Interestingly enough, some of the same people who wanted to legalize it and stood to gain from it were lobbying against commuting and reducing sentences. This was particularly troublesome as there were many cases where people were incarcerated for being found with minimal amounts of the substance. At the same time, people in official capacities (lawmakers, etc.) invested in the development of products, grow houses, and distribution models, generating a stream of income that was largely hidden from the general public. This is an example to illustrate the dichotomy that exists. It is less about your perspective on legalization or the debate about whether or not there should be consideration for the outcome of prior violations of law.

What you should observe is that we have something that has the potential for good, yet we held it back for quite a while. The system in existence jailed minority citizens at an inordinately higher rate in comparison to non-minorities. Had legalization occurred earlier, an infrastructure could have supported economic growth, and minorities might have been in a position to benefit from the cannabis industry. Ultimately, the legalization of cannabis with varied implementation standards exists across the country. It would have been the same if legalization had occurred years before. The difference is who would benefit from it. The same product and its derivatives are used in lotions, beverages, edible products, and recreational and medicinal items. It is the very same product that, when carried, purchased, and used, warranted jail time because it was illegal.

Let's look at the impact. People who were arrested for cannabis-related crimes carry a <u>record for life</u>, which in turn results in reduced employment opportunities. They are often stigmatized by the same people who utilize cannabis today for recreational and medicinal benefits. The connection to cannabis has significantly tainted the image of black and brown people, yet it is now acceptable and legal. The law has changed, but the stigma remains, along with the financial and social impact. It is also very clear to see that the now legal utilization extends across all communities, not just to communities of color.

Creating a differentiation between groups of people endangers humanity. Over time, judgment is placed and levied differently based on the person's identity and their connections to various groups. In addition to the collective and societal impact, the individual is wounded significantly as well. Everyone loses in the end. The soul is impacted by an imprint that has now been part of the DNA for multiple generations. For those who carry the stigma, they have an outward scarlet letter and an internal scar. The weight of the central soul is impacted as if a weight were placed on the unhealed side of the scale. Each time there is more inequality and injustice levied against people, it weighs heavily upon the soul. Because of the connection between those who share DNA, the impacts are far-reaching. The requirement to heal broadens as the perspectives of people, not just one person, have been impacted. Ultimately, the choice not to heal exacerbates the former wounds, and the central soul's health is further depressed.

Alcohol provides a good parallel. While it is legal, it is unlawful for anyone under 21 to purchase or drink alcohol. TV portrays teen and young adult parties where underage drinking is happening regularly.

The shows are even rated for teens. Underage drinking is glorified on TV. Shows portray the teens as being cool and having a good time while engaging in something illegal. In many cases, these parties occur in a home where access to alcohol is not protected.

For teens who have not fully developed their prefrontal cortex, temptation and encouragement are present in most of the things that they watch. The prefrontal cortex regulates decision-making, reasoning, and impulse management. It stands to reason that constant images of people engaging in underage drinking might be seen as socially acceptable, regardless of the law that is being broken.

Consider this parallel example. An 18-year-old college student is at a fraternity party where there is underage drinking. The student is caught drinking and faces discipline at school. Often, these incidents do not result in the authorities being notified. In this case, there was a fight, and the student was detained. He appears in court and waits for the Judge to decide about what is to come. Under the social acceptance of drinking, there is a tendency towards leniency. That leniency is not applied equally. It may be a slap on the wrist for some and a much more significant outcome for others. Bias and assumptions impact fair adjudication. It's evident that we see people differently. We look at others in ways that are not equal, even when the circumstances are the same.

Herein lies the heart of the problem. For us to be at our best, our souls need connectivity. The central soul is the sum of the parts. The center soul is in crisis simply because some people suffer significantly. Their suffering will impact the whole. Looking back at our two examples, we can imagine the halo of impact broader than those involved. Imagine there was a 20-year-old student in both examples, one with possession of cannabis and one intoxicated with alcohol, who were both arrested as both were crimes at the time of our example. The one who was intoxicated is released without any impact on their record. The person who had possession of cannabis was charged and jailed with a conviction on their record. The adjudication is only a part of the impact. For the 20-year-old released, there is a varying degree of impact and likely momentary suffering as they navigate the residual feelings and any stigma attached to the arrest. For the other student, their incarceration limits the type of work they can do upon release. There is an impact on the family financially, from the cost related to the case to the lost potential of wages for the length of time that they are unable to work due to their detainment, extending to the reduction in earning potential connected to the types of jobs that they would now be considered unqualified to do. This is an oversimplification of the issue, but it can be easily seen that when there is a differentiation of treatment, suffering follows. Pause for a moment to consider how you visualized this example. Be curious. What were your assumptions? Did you assume the race of either or both 20-year-old students? What gender did you assume? Were there physical characteristics that you assumed- height, build, etc? Did you dismiss the illegal alcohol use because even though the individual was underage, alcohol was legal where cannabis was not? Without judgment, take a moment to inter-rogate your biases. Is something illegal because it is illegal, or is it 'less' illegal because of a societal norm? How do you really think and feel?

In the same way, you create a picture in your mind, and biases play out wherever people make decisions and design solutions. This would be an excellent time to pause and journal about the varied emotions that arose for you in this section. What biases did you see in yourself? How do you feel about them? What concerns you about the central soul and how bias and suffering play a role? What do you want to do differently to encourage healing within and beyond yourself?

One of the reasons that making your personal reflections matters is that the further we believe we are from someone else's suffering, the less we feel compelled to do something about it. The larger the chasm between those who are healing and those who are suffering, the greater the pull on our central soul. Those who are struggling the most operate at further distances from the safety and acceptance of the central soul. The greater the distance between people, the longer the path back to operating as one soul. It has been established that the central soul creates access to the same emotions and energy generated by our experiences individually and collectively. It also means that empathy, understanding, consideration, love, patience, fairness, and justice for all are required. **As one suffers, so will another.** Your suffering may not come in the same form as someone else's, but you will experience it. It may not be by the same hand, but it will come nonetheless.

It is time to take on the mindset that what we are creating has a broad impact, even when it does not look like it. Our minds begin to shift as we consider the impact of experiences that may not mirror the things that happen in our own lives, but have the ability to impact us nonetheless. Imagine a farm collective. If everyone works at levels that they set on their own without agreement and a shared goal, it is very probable that there will be some inequity. There might be a soil-borne disease on one farm and an irrigation issue on another. If one crop is not productive, they might be missing all of the items they planned to share. The following season, those who struggled might have the best harvest, and perhaps your crop yielded 1/3 of the expected amount. The beauty of the collective is that there is the opportunity to support one another with the recognition that there is an ebb and flow.

We were designed to live in community with one another. We will return to that model eventually, and it is important to realize that you are not now, nor were you ever, living in a world where your choices and decisions only had an impact on yourself.

Jane Elliott, an educator whose work centers on ending racism and discrimination and creating awareness, has completed several studies and exercises that help people understand discrimination.

> In one powerful session, **Jane Elliott** asked non-Black participants to stand if they would be willing to trade places with Black people and live their experiences. No one stood. Not surprisingly, the participants did not want to trade places. This example, and Elliott's well-known blue eyes/brown eyes experiment, reveals a powerful truth about the central soul. There was a clear recognition that an undesirable experience was occurring, whether in the brown-eyed group or in the experience of being Black in America. *(Source: Elliott, Jane. Blue Eyed. Directed by Bertram Verhaag, 1996.)*

As a collective, we know that inequity exists across the world. Gender inequality exists on every continent. It extends to working rights, pay equity, and social standing. There are ongoing risks to women's health, extending from fundamental human rights to protect their bodies to the ongoing debate around a woman's right to choose. To sum it up, there are varying risks to simply being female.

Pause for a moment and consider this. Women bring life into the world. They have an incredibly precious role as nurturers during pregnancy and as a child is born. Regardless of the relationship, every human has a woman's body as a part of the gift of their life. As the chosen gender to deliver life into the world, why should men determine so many decisions made regarding their bodies and livelihood? This is a philosophical question for your consideration. The ability to bring life into the world is unique to women. Why is there a less-than-equal standard for thought leadership as well as tangible rights?

It is interesting to note that there are studies about gender in the media that point back to the stereotypes of gender roles appearing early in childhood. The stereotypes related to gender are portrayed in the media to further support the current views and create differentiation when people behave in a way that does not align with the stereotype. Objectification and over-sexualization of women in the media are rampant. There is a clear juxtaposition between being the precious being within whom life is created and messages that describe women as being lesser in value or contribution.

Objectification Theory directs our attention to some specific impacts of the types of representation seen in the media. Fredrickson and Roberts suggest that the objectification of women creates conditions where shame and anxiety can evolve. They contrast that with several mental health risks that include eating disorders and depression. Their work identifies a behavior that is specific to women, resulting in monitoring and excessive observation of their bodies, which leads to shaming and their own self-objectification.

Ultimately, how women are portrayed in the media has to align with treatment in the real world for it to be credible. If there was no interest in seeing women portrayed in a way that minimized their contributions, objectified them, and diminished their value, it simply would not make good entertainment. Think back for a moment at a show that portrayed something or a group of people in a way that was misaligned with your core values or beliefs. Did you watch the show? How willing are you to stand by what you believe to be right? The more that we allow groups of people to be treated poorly and misrepresented, the more healing we need as a society. Before you think, "Well, women allow themselves to be seen that way," or excuse behavior because of their dress, take a pause. Over time, the things we tell ourselves that we cannot change become our reality. They become things that we accept and that becomes our norm. Norms are not synonymous with the best and highest interests of humanity. In every situation, healing has to happen before it can happen between people.

Foreign companies are extracting resources from many countries without committing to improving the quality-of-life experience of those who work and live in the local community. Children are being enslaved, separated from their families, and unable to attend school or worse. The issue of human trafficking is growing at an alarming rate around the world, threatening families and the safety of our children.

These are some of the examples of conditions in this world that we know are occurring, yet are not eradicated. Humanity has grown to turn a blind eye to situations until they "hit home." There is knowledge that something wrong is happening, yet at the same time, if a person can depersonalize it, they can minimize feelings attached to it.

As a collective, humanity works to avoid pain for itself but has grown more tolerant of it being inflicted on others. The central soul grounds us in our interconnectedness. It says that if one is suffering, all will suffer. The disconnect is grounded in the distance between us and the lack of empathy. When we are separated from the experiences of others, it is more difficult for us to understand their plight, which in turn makes us more apathetic. This state of mind works in opposition to moving toward a solution that will support everyone.

There is a saying, "A rising tide lifts all boats," a phrase popularized by President John F. Kennedy. That 'Rising Tide' is our collective healing. We heal and impact the central soul when we work individually on our healing journey. Setting intentions on healing our lineage and supporting others on their healing journey are significant contributions to the central soul's health. As a result, we begin to experience life collectively as our creator intended it.

Chapter Pearls

- Humanity is the collective. We are connected by the creator's design, and we make up the Central Soul.

- Every time we focus our intentions on healing, we begin casting positive energy for ourselves and the collective.

- Unexplored and unaddressed bias presents a risk to the collective.

- We can no longer feign ignorance about the disparity of treatment that exists. Healing is required, which will require action by the collective.

Journal Prompts

- How did this chapter open your eyes to assumptions and biases that are familiar to you?

- What can you do to understand the suffering of others better? How might it help you connect with your own suffering?

- What commitment can you make to your healing journey and to support the healing of others to positively impact the central soul?

Chapter Seven

Health of the Central Soul

We are working towards the health of our connected soul, aptly named the Central Soul. The central soul is not a catchphrase designed to illustrate a point that doesn't exist. The central soul is real, which is why healing progress can be slow and limited. The advancement of the collective is connected. Consider the image of a continuum where people operate at the extremes, such as the far left and far right of the range. When people are disconnected, evidenced by their distance from others, the impact is greater than it is on a single individual. In addition to the direct impact on people, a residual impression is left on the systems that guide the world.

For example, there has been an ongoing conversation in the United States surrounding the impending retirement of the baby boomers and the impact it will have on Social Security. Generation X has been in the workforce for about 25-50 years, depending on their birth year. Those with earlier birth years have been contributing to Social Security for closer to 40-55 years. There is a credible concern and high likelihood that the program will not be able to support those born in the 1960s to early 1980s range. Citizens are paying into the federal program in advance of utilizing the funds. This system helps support those who are exiting the workforce. Several factors suggest that the same people may not be able to draw against the funds that they contributed.

There is an impact because of the number of people that have to be served in the generation that precedes the one that is now paying into the system by the largest number of people. In the same way, there's a drag on the Social Security system because of the massive number of people who are a part of the baby boomer generation, which means the pressure is on Generation X and millennials, followed by Generation Y (Millennials), and so forth. The burden on Generation Y is big; they will bear the brunt of the work because they have the most working years left. This, of course, is contingent on whether or not the system exists. There is a possibility that the current system will be dismantled and replaced with a new system.

This situation provides a tangible example of what happens when conflicting needs or issues occur. In relation to the central soul, there is a pulling at both ends of the spectrum. The tension represents the competing needs and desires of humanity. Any reasonable solution requires that there be openness to concession. There will always be issues for mankind to explore and resolve. Utilizing a different perspective is required to identify solutions that best serve the whole. There will always be a need for people to consider the impact beyond themselves. HEALING will always be required. The healing must be born from a commitment between people to do what is right for the collective community.

This idea of healing our central soul is critical. It is part of the individual's plight and the collective's journey. Explore the imagery in this example. An individual has been intentional about their healing and is actively engaging in the work. They are progressing towards their best life, represented by them floating up to the top of a body of water, where they were once submerged. The individual rises towards the top, only to find their body still several feet from the top. They realize that there is a cement block tied to their ankle. With the greatest force imaginable, the individual cannot move closer to the goal of living their best life. The cement block directly opposes their desire to break through the water's surface. They are faced with a decision: should they continue to fight to get free or float back down to the level of the cement block and try to remove it?

It becomes evident that in either scenario, the person will likely drown. They begin to realize that whether they choose to ignore the issue, attempt to free their ankle, or select other options that further exacerbate the conditions, it is nearly impossible to emerge from the water. The conditions hinder their ability to move, even though they have done the work and are clear about their goal.

This is the dilemma that faces humanity concerning the central soul. There is no way to disconnect yourself from it. You are connected. All of humanity is connected. The level at which you experience the connection through your consciousness or the divine is specific to where you are in the moment; in your acknowledgment that the central soul is connected to you and everyone else across humanity. Armed with the revelation of truth, you can shift your attention to identifying what you will do to strengthen the health of the central soul.

In the example, the individual cannot fully realize their goals because of the weight of the cement block. The cement block is the pull of the collective on the central soul. Those who choose not to heal create backward momentum for the whole, creating the pull on the spectrum, with collective consideration and healing creating the pull in the opposite direction. Individually, you find yourself with choices. The divine choice is to move beyond human selfishness and ego.

People generally form perceptions about who are "good people" and who are "bad people." Similarly, there are perceptions about a person's value. People are inherently good. Some choices lead to actions we can define as "good" and "bad," but it is not an accurate assessment to label a person as bad or good. Value speaks to contribution and even impact. The interesting thing is that you can't truly see the value of a person. It is impossible to accurately assess someone based on their past experiences. The truth is that once they are in a healed state and walking in the purpose for which they were designed, their value (contribution) is almost immeasurable. You simply cannot see it by looking at someone in the midst of suffering and seeking healing. When people begin the process of healing, they return to the core of who they (truly) are intended to be. As they heal and begin to live into their purpose, you can begin to envision the potential impact they can deliver.

Of course, there is always a choice, and some people will not choose to stay on the full path to their ultimate self. Regardless of what happens in the long term, making assumptions about people in the dark spaces of unhealed conditions is unfair. It can be compared to judging a newborn baby on what they will be in this world based on their dexterity at birth. Even assessments of their ability to form sentences or their attention span cannot fully capture their potential. We would not judge a baby's brilliance based solely on their ability to observe a thing for more than a few seconds without looking away from the stimulus. You get the picture.

In the simplicity of the examples of newborns, it is clear that we would not judge them in those situations. However, it is more difficult to see another adult or even an older child as needing the same time to learn and grow as a newborn. That is the thing. Healing is new for many, especially at the depth that is required for the time that we are in. This is one of the foundational reasons to treat others with grace and consideration. In the same way, empathy is present for the newborn; similar grace and understanding should be exhibited to others.

The way people have grown to treat one another is not grounded in empathy, nor does it resemble the golden rule. Compassion is absent from the collective's behavior. Humanity has taken on behavior that states that it is ok to treat others in a way that people would never readily accept for themselves. This acceptance of maligned treatment is deteriorating mankind's condition. This is a result of unhealed conditions. The behavior of acceptance of poor treatment stems from the devaluing of self and treatment by others that mirrors the same. When people are oppressed and marginalized, their self-worth is diminished. As a result of treatment that minimizes the value of a person, they begin to look to external places to validate their worth. It is like saying that as a result of how you have been treated, you must find someone to now affirm what you know is true about yourself.

The best way to counter the connection to others' validation is to heal the relationship to your own worthiness. The act of valuing yourself, your thoughts, and your perspective is an act of love. It includes actively releasing the desire to fit in to "the way things are" as you envelop your truth. It ushers forth healing that helps you to see yourself more clearly. Over time, your inner voice becomes stronger, and boundaries are drawn. Healing is the key. Without the inner work to counter the treatment that people often experience, the real lesson is missed. When you realize that how people interact with you provides an opportunity for you to see how well you care for yourself, things change. As you begin to see situations as opportunities for growth, the desire to respond from a place of hurt lessens over time. That is a pivotal part of the collective healing journey.

The world and you are depending on your continued choice to heal. You are connected whether you want to be or not. This is a hard truth. Whatever you do has an impact on the collective, which means the choices of others have an impact on the collective as well. The central soul will ebb and flow based on where people are in relation to themselves and others. The more individuals choose to heal themselves, the healthier the central soul. By choosing to work to strengthen one another, there is a reduction in divisiveness, division, hatred, misunderstanding, and avoidance. Unchecked, these emotions and subsequent behaviors will permeate the central soul. The repercussions of these feelings create an energetic vibration that affects all people.

You might be thinking, "What do I do?" When people decide that they simply don't like other people or when they've chosen to keep resources to themselves, there is an impact on the collective. When a "safe haven" and protective gate are created around individuals, the residual impact from avoidance permeates the central soul. The central soul's state is also subject to the generation of fear and other feelings.

Some people may be okay with the existence of others as long as it requires nothing from them, but there is no way to fully detach yourself from the whole. Regardless of the journey, no one has reached where they are today without the impact or connection to others. Their experiences may be varied, from child-rearing to mentorship, but ultimately, there has been some connection. People may have lacked the feeling of belonging or, in some cases, may have experienced extreme preference. The desire to separate oneself from others has varied origins. Ultimately, the disconnect creates a lasting impact on the individual and the collective.

Consider a large corporation with thousands of employees. The knowledge of and availability of resources are connected to the corporate culture. In some organizations, there are resources within the corporation that are not secret, but they're quietly kept. The company may require certain criteria before the resources are made available to an employee. Perhaps access requires the connection to a mentor or sponsor as the gatekeeper to those resources. Many employees may have no idea that these resources even exist. That is a challenge. Some employees would not ask for access to the resources simply because they are unaware of their existence. Others might be misdirected simply because the leaders they seek information from are unaware of the resources.

Ultimately, this results in a workforce that is not operating at its optimum level. They could do more with full access to all resources. In the same way, individuals cannot have the impact they were designed to have on the balance of the collective without the health of the central soul. There must be a change for people to operate at their best. Healing is required. There is something very big here for you to explore around your ways of connecting and how you see the connectedness of others.

Much of this chapter has focused on seeing the connection to others. It is essential to recognize that your personal commitment to your own healing and growth is required.

The beauty of this book is that you are beginning to truly see how often you consider the actions and behavior of others. You have learned to constantly look outward at others. In and of itself, the process of looking outward is beneficial. The pure intent is to see a mirror on the face of others that reflects back to you. You should see yourself in others, see the frailty, missteps, successes, and worthiness. When you look outward, a connection should be created. This has been misdirected to avoid the requirement of seeing one's own truth. You cannot heal without being willing to see yourself. You cannot connect without seeing the similarities between yourself and others. These connections were created to bind people together, not to create an unforgiving hierarchy where people constantly look for a group to be at the bottom. Don't fear others; fear the divide between people. The divide is detrimental to the establishment of the whole, the central soul.

Admittedly, the concept of the central soul feels complex and perhaps a bit unfair. You have been conditioned to move in the world with less regard for others than what is required for collective progress and healing. For some, the opposite is true. You may have focused more on the plight of others than on your own personal state and healing journey. Whichever is more aligned with your truth, be sure that your personal healing and the healing of the collective matter.

In summary, you are connected to one another. The healing journey you have begun will impact your life and the collective. As you engage with others along your life path, your choices and decisions will intersect with theirs. Your level of healing and self-awareness can support the healing of other individuals as well as the collective. The state of the central soul also impacts your life, evidenced by the way others engage with you and the collective behavior within the world.

Now that you have a deeper understanding of the One Soul and the connectivity of humanity, it is time to take a moment to allow information and feelings to emerge. Journaling is a great way to capture how you feel in this moment. You might find that sitting quietly or meditating in this moment would provide even more clarity for you.

The application of the wisdom shared in this chapter is the foundation for the balance of this book and, quite frankly, for humanity's plight. The range of feelings you are experiencing is welcome. Conflicting and contradicting information may arise. That is to be welcomed, too. Processing feelings and thoughts is healing, and as you know, Healing is Required.

The Heart of the Central Soul

At the heart of it all, the grounding force is love. Love is a shared emotion, like most emotions. The feeling of love swells within one individual. They look to radiate that love to another person. Love that is generated between two people makes twice the impact. When that love radiates beyond them, there can be an exponential effect. This compounding of love's impact can generate healing far beyond its origin.

At the core of humanity, there are shared needs. Love is the foundation.

Denial of the value of others is a denial of self-worth.

Rejection of others leads to rejection and loathing of self.

Separation of people leads to separation of self from the whole

Once division between people occurs, simultaneous healing becomes the mechanism for reconnection. Love is the only force that can heal in the midst of hurt, pain, and destruction.

Many who have chosen to destroy the connection between humanity suffer from the onset of their behavior. They have not known love. They have denied love. They have chased away love. They have rejected love.

They cannot heal on their own, and they will not heal on their own. They cannot undo their actions without the capacity and desire to love.

So, you **must** love them.

It may seem difficult, but love is the only way to change a heart.

This is why cycles of destruction persist, because love has been pushed aside. Control, anger, and manipulation breed their offspring: more control, anger, manipulation, and hatred. You cannot counter divisive behavior with more of the same behavior. To break the cycle, love is required. The core of the central soul is love; it is the heart.

When circumstances occur, people react or respond. Those who have not experienced the true and genuine love available to them will often continue to choose the one that has brought them pain. This pattern continues until all they know is pain. It is difficult to remember that love was ever an option.

Remember that your hearts are connected. They all began beating with purity and are filled with love. Choices and circumstances created the distance in behavior. To love those who are in pain and suffering will always be an honorable choice.

To love others does not mean to forego the love of self. On the contrary, it means loving yourself enough to choose to see the soul inside another that is starving for love. Love will always overcome. Love will breed more love. Love will heal all that is broken. The question is, will you choose love?

Chapter Pearls

- The healing must be born from a commitment between people to do what is right on behalf of the collective community.

- The central soul is influenced by healing. When more people invest in their individual healing, the collective is impacted through that healing.

- Love is always the answer.

Journal Prompts

- How do you contribute to the health of the Central Soul?

- What things will you do to create more love for yourself and others?

Chapter Eight

The Power of Integration

Integration is a way of life. We are constantly melding without realizing it. Integration is a critical part of the learning process. New concepts and ideas must be connected to other information to organize, store, and use it most effectively.

The new information that we take in is integrated with what exists. Connections are made between new and old information. In some cases, integration may not refer to something new. Two concepts that are separate from each other can be integrated as well. With the utilization of new perspectives, you recognize the correlation and the necessity for them to become one. It becomes a part of how we derive meaning and ultimately impacts the quality of our existence. You become expansive when you can accept the correlation between thoughts, experiences, and concepts.

Integration extends beyond the organization of information. As it pertains to people, integration means operating in all parts of yourself. As integration is evolutionary, it is important to note that there is no specific point where we reach completion. Integration is always ongoing as we evolve our understanding and grow in perspective.

People who are focused on integrating self are on a journey to be at their highest and best possible self. Healing is required as they walk their path to unlock all of who they are. It requires that they explore and understand things about themselves where there may have been a block in the past.

The need to integrate may arise around areas that have been difficult to accept, even though there may be awareness that they exist. Integration requires openness and a decision to live life from a place of true and genuine authenticity. It propels the person to lean into the fullness of who they are. When integration is happening, people observe shifts in their behavior and mindset.

For example, one might observe a person bringing their personal philosophy into every area of their life. If they desire to create more love in the world, they will operate from a place of love in everything they do. Whether they are parenting, at work, serving in the community, working the polls during election season, or simply grocery shopping, they lead with love. They find ways to pour love out into the world. An integrated person experiences and shares love in every area of their life.

The example of a person not fully integrated is very familiar to everyone. Much of humanity operates in a non-integrated fashion. In this case, you would observe a person operating differently across the areas of their life. You might see them operating from a place of love when they are in their religious ceremonies, church, and perhaps with their family. The disconnect is evidenced when they navigate other areas of their life. For example, the corporate arena, political realm, or a service provider like a hospital are places that are likely misaligned with the person's value of love. Their approach in those places is to behave in a way that doesn't allow them to show the principle of love that they value so deeply. As a result, they may show up in a way that feels cold and aloof.

Even though they may be feeling love on the inside, they work very hard to keep it so submerged or suppressed. Suppression is a choice that works in opposition to integration. The individual's choice to allow their personal philosophy or the value of love to be suppressed results in a disconnect for the person. They may be successful with navigating the environments, but they are sacrificing themselves to do so.

The choice has a range of impacts that occur below the water line, which are not readily seen but are significant to the full picture. Selecting "sides" of self sends a clear message that it is not ok to be fully themselves. That statement and the connected behaviors contribute to the deterioration of the self. Worthiness and other beliefs are tied to how we view ourselves. The repetition of messaging that only parts of the self are acceptable or welcome continues to distance a person from their truth and their expansiveness.

Integration matters. You are meant to be your full self at all times. You were designed to walk in the fullness of all that you are. Integrated people behave and move in ways that honor what they have the potential to give to the world. One's experiences are strengthened by showing up as one's full self. The people around you are blessed when you show up as the true and authentic you. All of the facets of who you are have value. Your integration of self allows you to create a deep and meaningful impact in varied circumstances. The full version of you always makes a difference.

Reflect on a time when you or someone else showed up as a shell of themselves. Perhaps in a meeting, the individual held back ideas or creative discourse that could have shifted the direction of a decision. Those moments are pivotal for the individual and others.

Progress can be lost when one who has been gifted the ability to see something from a different perspective is not free to express an unrepresented position. In business, discourse from as many sides as there are customers is meaningful when making decisions. Imagine you are the person holding a million-dollar idea in your mind. One person operating from a non-integrated place can choose to hold back a thought or idea that would have triggered a conversation that created validity for your million-dollar solution. It is entirely possible that both of you could have left the meeting without sharing what was placed inside of you for that very moment.

Living from an integrated state allows you to show up in full. Some question if it is genuinely ok for everyone to show up fully. The real question is whether or not the full self is "acceptable" in the environment or culture. If you return to the basis of our human truth, there are several things to consider. Showing up in full is relative. Today's version of you is different from the one you were yesterday or last year. Growth happens as perspective is broadened. Everyone can only show up to the fullest of who they are at that moment.

Control looks like discouraging people from being their whole selves. Love looks like creating an environment where it is welcome, and the norms established for that space are inclusive and consistently applied. This provides a great barometer to help one measure their growth. Control is connected to fear, more specifically, an effort to avoid the things that one is fearful of experiencing. The root of fear, of course, is found in areas that require healing. If you know that whatever happens in life creates an opportunity for you to grow, regardless of whether or not you want to experience the challenge, you allow yourself to keep going. Control aims to avoid and minimize risk, often eliminating the opportunity to fall and rise again. Looking beyond the individual, we see that people desire to control others for various reasons. Some may stem from a desire to keep others safe. It may be rooted in a choice to allow people to experience only what one has deemed acceptable for themselves. In any case, this is fear-based, not focused on growth and love. When we heal, we recognize the benefit of the experiences that have helped us grow. The appetite for growth, risk, and what some may perceive as failure grows stronger. We understand that growth and healing are connected.

Often, the desire for control shows up as a quest for perfectionism. The mindset emerging from the pain of old wounds begins to form around the idea that if we are "perfect," we can avoid the pain of failure. The word failure can be replaced by any adverse condition that feels pertinent to the individual. Some people spend a lot of time creating the perfect conditions to ensure nothing goes wrong. Imagine working at creating the perfect scenario to avoid pain and then feeling it anyway. It is even more painful than if the time spent creating the controlled environment was *squandered* on something like fun! In truth, the energy expelled in control is significant. When successful in avoiding what is seen as an adverse condition, the person is rewarded. The success encourages them to do more to control the conditions around them. Over time, it becomes part of how they operate.

In scenarios like this, what is often missed is the inherent stress of trying to control everything. Frequently, the person will spend time planning, orchestrating care for others, and activating the perfect plan. When this emerges as a pattern, it becomes a way of being. When multiple disappointments threaten the way of being, the person begins to struggle. The desire to get it right begins to supersede the initial outcome that they desired. After a while, the standard of perfectionism is set. Often, these same individuals begin to use the lens they have created to evaluate their way of operating in the world for others. They begin to expect perfection from the people around them. The expectation that one is perfect and without the need for growth is false. Everyone in every environment has some level of growth to experience. Recognizing the need for growth in others should be a regular reflection of your own growth, spanning your opportunities and successes as you have grown.

It is important to remember that norms are guides, not laws. Thank goodness this is so. If norms had no flexibility, innovation would be at risk. We need to think more broadly. Some of the best ideas come from diverse experiences. Take fashion designers, for example. Their creativity often draws from nature's textures and colors. Inspiration frequently originates from outside the industry, connecting seemingly unrelated ideas, textures, materials, and styles to create something new. Embracing creativity should be the norm, not only welcoming it when it fits in with what is perceived as the norm.

Fashion has often stepped outside of the established norms, successfully so, and it has been celebrated. Ask yourself, "Why is it different when someone veers outside the norm?" What makes it acceptable for some people to be significantly different from the norm?

Pause and think about three people in business who regularly step outside the norm. Are they extremely wealthy? The answer is likely yes. Shall the conclusion be drawn that if someone is perceived to be of less means, they should succumb to the norm? Is your conclusion that they are less capable of creating? When societal norms are made, it is important to examine what is said through exceptions as well as the establishment of the norm. If a norm is created to encourage connectivity and consistency, why would exceptions be made for some groups of people? In this case, the super-wealthy might be the exception.

When taking a step back, it's clear that this journey has been about understanding the need for healing. We see the "why" at individual, familial, community, and collective human levels. Healing impacts all these areas. To heal, we must integrate different parts of ourselves, addressing various unhealed behaviors, thoughts, and memories that keep us stagnant. While healing, one aspect may bring slight progress, but full healing is necessary to live a healthy, fulfilling life. This journey benefits us and sheds light on the impact our healing has on future generations and those in our close communities, including coworkers and fellow members of our groups or organizations. Ultimately, we can begin to see how our healing impacts the world.

How The Need for Healing Is Exposed

Everyone will experience identifying places that are unhealed along life's journey. Healing occurs in pieces, not all at one time. The imagery of waves washing up on the shoreline helps to illustrate the concept. Imagine the water coming to reveal places where Healing Is Required. As the water pulls back from the shore, you can clearly see the condition of the shoreline and the sand. When the next wave comes in, the layers of the sand shift again, and more is revealed. The tide is responsive to the time of day, among other factors. As the tide becomes still, there is time for settling before the next set of waves. As things are revealed to you, the decision must be made to heal or to ignore the need. Once the decision to heal is made, you work when the tide is out to address the issues beneath the surface. The tide will begin to move in the next cycle, causing the waves to roll up to the shore again and to reveal more areas of "healing."

Healing in pieces is a beautiful thing. Attempting to heal everything at once would be overwhelming, and people would likely give up.

When situations are overwhelming, people often give in because that is how the human mind works. The mind says, "This is not safe." Healing in phases provides a manageable amount of introspection, exploration, and decision-making/action. You can choose to heal the parts of ourselves at the right time and then integrate the healing into who we are. Healing is connected. The mere act of integrating places where you have experienced healing already improves the other areas where there are things to be addressed. The improved emotional and mental health conditions impact the other areas where healing is required. Those unhealed areas receive the benefits that result from the healing and integration. The impact on the areas that are not fully healed is significant. It does not negate the need for healing specific to the root of those areas. However, the individual is in an even better position to heal.

Let's go back to the example of love. Envision someone who experiences love in their home social circle but not at work. The experience of love is not present in ministry or philanthropic endeavors. It is not present in the outer circle of people who are categorized as acquaintances. Likely, they are not open to receiving or expressing love to those outside of their inner circle. If the individual only allows love to show through with those who are truly closest to them, they will likely only receive love from those same people. They would miss the experience of giving and receiving more love. In fact, choosing to pour love into acquaintances is one of the most beautiful gifts. Those individuals have the opportunity to experience more of the person, and they grow from giving without expecting love in return. Keeping that example in mind, consider the shift that can occur as they heal the places in themselves around expressing love. As they heal the places inside that are permeating the boundaries around the importance of love, they begin to understand that love is needed and that they desire to be loved.

The integration of the healing work unfolds the importance of love. The person begins to see why love matters and is needed in all areas of life. They begin to allow the value of love to be present at work and in relationships with acquaintances. The person begins to experience the feeling of alignment and recognizes the improvement across once-segmented parts of their existence. Healing shifts their perspective, and eventually, they build comfort in expressing love.

They begin to pour love out without expecting anything in return. Their broadened perspective enables them to understand that love is a gift that they give to others and to themselves. Love can be given freely because they know the source of it. In recognizing the Divine, who is love, they understand they will never be depleted. There is always an abundance of love.

The self-talk of the person sounds somewhat like this:

"I know who I am in connection to the divine. I can give love without worrying about whether it will be returned. I can allow myself to be vulnerable in spaces where I may not see an immediate return. I can accept that sometimes I won't experience love returning from where I deposited it. My integrated self says that as long as I meet my need to be present and spread love, I will do my part."

Consider the disconnect that they likely feel if the way they lead with love is not a fit for the culture at their current employer. They may conclude that the disconnect is polarizing. Through their reevaluation, they realize that they don't particularly like elements of their job. This is powerful. Each time they go to work, the truth settles in more deeply. They realize they do not enjoy being in that environment and are not experiencing love. That acknowledgment helps them realize they are standing in the truth of love each time they go to their workplace. Going to the workplace does not make them love themselves; on the contrary, it is because they love themselves that they go to the workplace despite the misalignment. As this recognition becomes more pronounced, they begin to see and experience the disconnect. The goal is to work through the misalignment once they explore it to determine the root cause. They understand that they must embrace showing up from a place of love and accepting that people may not return it. They can strengthen their resolve by pouring love into the workplace, knowing it will positively impact others, even though there may be some personal disconnect between them. Eventually, after changing how they engage with others at work, the person will come to a moment where they might choose to change their work because it is not aligned.

People make the decision to move in accordance with the truth within when they recognize their sovereignty. Once the healing process has begun, acknowledging truth becomes a core mission. Typically, part of the truth that has been revealed indicates that more healing must be done. This serves as an indicator that healing is indeed a journey. As a result of healing, you will become stronger and clearer about who you are at the core. Healing helps people to truly see who they are. It is like watching a lotus open. There is even more goodness inside to be explored as you evolve.

So, how do you integrate your healing? One moment at a time. Perspective plays a significant role in the healing process. **Perspective** matters, and it **can change everything**. How you see yourself, who you believe you are, and what you tell yourself all have significant implications on your healing experiences. The narrative that you are accepting about yourself makes all the difference in how you experience life. To integrate healing, you must be open to exploring all of yourself. Integrating the healing means you will evolve your way of thinking and behaving. It is important to see yourself as a whole. Your healing will impact all of you, and it sets the tone for releasing the practice of showing up in different ways and other spaces. When you see yourself as a whole being, you give yourself grace for the journey of healing. Gratitude becomes a core part of how you see the world and operate within it. You work to build yourself up through trust and loving yourself. This sets the foundation for healing. Then, the work of integration begins. Integration is how you bring those things together.

If you were healing a childhood trauma, you would focus on processing feelings, emotions, and experiences resulting from the trauma. You might be working through things like PTSD, anxiety, and perhaps a feeling of abandonment. In healing the trauma, you would likely identify feelings of neglect, unworthiness, or even a lack of advocacy as you move into narratives that emerged from the trauma. You identify the areas that are being healed. Integration requires you to look across your life and say, "Where else does this exist? How has the mindset that I've had connected to the experiences or responses to other situations? What is the impact of the current narrative compared to what the new narrative will open up for me?" The exploration of the connections is one of the most powerful experiences that occurs in the healing journey. When you can see themes, patterns, and mindsets, the doorway to who you truly are opens up even wider.

For example, it is entirely possible for someone to have a difficult relationship with the opposite gender at work and experience a similar struggle with the same gender in relationships within their personal life. At the onset, the individual might have believed the issue was rooted in relation to the opposite sex in a work environment. The information about difficulty relating to the same gender in social environments suggests that the issue may not be gender related at all.

A reasonable hypothesis could be that they struggle with connection in general and that it is difficult for them to build a sense of trust. Trust is a likely root of the issue, given the minimal information in our hands. As humans, our edict is to truly love one another and trust only in the Divine, the root of higher truth. However, in the foundational experiences, what we would consider to be human trust is likely lacking. This is where the desire to trust people is substituted with "I'm trusting in the divine, and I choose to believe that you are going to do right by me" as the core expectation.

Let's delve into this topic further. At first glance, it might seem that relationships with co-workers can't possibly affect how you see your partner or friends. However, that's not true. Our minds constantly make connections, mark experiences as safe, and encourage us to re-peat familiar patterns. If you consistently avoid speaking up, it might be due to a fear of retaliation, dismissal, or disrespect. This hesitation can hinder your professional growth. While your non-work relation-ships might initially seem unaffected, subtle changes can occur. For instance, if your partner starts to think or say things that differ from your expectations, you might withdraw from sharing your perspective to protect yourself.

Consider a scenario where your co-worker treats you exceptionally well—perhaps they bring you coffee daily and assist with your pro-jects. Subconsciously, you might begin to expect this same level of support at home. If your spouse, who is equally busy, doesn't meet these new expectations, it could create tension. Without realizing it, you might start linking the positive treatment at work to your home life, expecting similar dynamics.

These connections often form unconsciously. You might not even realize you're comparing your work experiences with your home life. Integration is key here. By examining these behavioral patterns, you can start to change them and operate in a way that lets your best self shine. This process will help you identify, understand, and alter the patterns that have been holding you back, allowing for personal growth both at work and at home.

In order to integrate, people must be open to the idea of there being unhealed places inside themselves. Leaving these places unhealed threatens everything for the person, from health to purpose to joy. It may be funny to be this far into the book and talk about the openness to see the unhealed places. Sometimes, people pause their reading once taking action becomes the obvious next step. You should know before you move into the next chapters that consequences result from avoiding healing. Understand what is hanging in the balance. Your healing is required for you to live the life you desire. There is also a residual impact on the broader community that will be addressed in a later chapter.

Integration is required in order for you to have the best outcome on your healing journey. You really can't navigate without it. As you look across the patterns you're experiencing in your life, it should become natural for you to explore an area where you want to grow and heal. It should also help you see other places where the same mindset could benefit you. You can choose to believe that all of the experiences and challenges that you've been through in your lifetime are strengthening you for the path ahead.

Consider the notion that those things were simply lessons and challenges so that you would experience the revelation of your character. These things had to occur so that you would understand who you are. This knowledge was given to you so that you would be prepared for what is ahead. Freedom and truth are found when you choose to believe that the things that have happened in your life are supporting you on the path ahead. This is the belief that life is unfolding for you and your best experience on your journey. Take your power back. Accept and own the choice to shift your perspective. Often, people unknowingly surrender their power because of how they act and think. When experiences in the past, albeit painful and disappointing, capture your energy in waves of anger and frustration, you allow your power to stay there. It is given away willingly- simply because the choice is made to be stuck in anger and frustration.

Believing in the power and alignment of lessons as support on the journey is required. At least, it is required if you want to live a more remarkable life. Be encouraged to let go more than you hold on. Release and forgive things more frequently and readily. Choose to keep the lessons and let go of what and why. The real personal power is present in your choice to use the lessons as fuel for your growth.

This moment is perfect for reflecting. What choices will you make to support and protect your growth? What correlations can you identify in areas you want to heal as you think about integrating healing? What do you believe about the experiences you have had? Did life happen for you or to you? What commitments will you make to yourself?

Chapter Pearls

- People focused on integrating self are on a journey to be at the highest and best self possible.

- Patterns of control and perfectionism are clues that healing is required.

- An evolution of your personal perspective and vision of self is critical for integrating your healing.

Journal Prompts

- How has life happened for you?

- What could it mean for you to reframe past experiences that you previously felt happened to you rather than for your growth?

Chapter Nine

Taking Aligned Action

P erhaps the most difficult challenge we face is moving from knowledge to action. Any delays we experience can stymie growth. Your decisions about what to do with this information are important. They matter to you as well as to the world. Choosing inaction is to choose not to heal. Choosing not to heal yourself leaves the collective open and exposed to the current circumstances we see in the world.

> "Imagine for a moment that all you had to do was focus on your own healing, and you could change the world."

Imagine for a moment that all you had to do was focus on your own healing, and you could change the world. That is essentially where we sit today. There is no intention to oversimplify things; however, individual healing leads to collective healing. As you truly embrace your highest self, you will desire to do more to help the collective heal.

Think about the most phenomenal meal you had in the last 30 days. You can remember it immediately because there is a connection to something that brings you joy. It may have been the food, company, or ambiance that made it stand out in your mind. Would you recommend the meal to others? Perhaps share the recipe or the address of the restaurant? People like to share things that connect to great experiences. When you experience something that brings you joy, it is natural to want to share that with others. In the same way, your healing experiences will make you so energized that you want to help other people on the path to their own experience.

The beauty in the desire to share is that the resulting effort is how we change the world. If your energy around your own personal healing intensifies as you experience the resulting changes, you will be transformed. Your transformation is public and influences the interactions that you have with others. The interactions cultivate curiosity, opening the space for dialogue about what is different. Your shift, experiences, tools, and resources are natural pieces to share with others. As a result, the person wants to help others experience the freedom and abundant life that is present when we are healed. Ultimately, the desire to heal and live in our purpose is how the world shifts.

As with anything, the opposite is also true. When the masses choose to avoid healing, humanity experiences the cyclical darkness present today. Misalignment with our purpose, coupled with trauma and unhealed wounds, leaves humanity engaging like ticking timebombs.

Anger and rage have found their home in people. Anger generates more anger. Deescalating anger and similar emotions requires a place of absorption. When someone behaves in anger, and it is returned to them, it generates even more anger, and the cycle continues. Anger does not require that the original stimulus be present. You might find that your anger after an argument with your spouse results in arguments with your co-workers or children. If there is a way to absorb the anger in love and understanding, the anger will begin to subside. Think of healing and the resulting energy of love, joy, and acceptance as the kryptonite for anger. Essentially, the energy of anger will dissipate if people remain in the place of love as they receive those with anger.

It makes sense for you to question why you would want to meet anger with love. The human way is to return emotion with the same type of emotion, matching the energy level. While that may be what feels "normal" to do, it does not create the outcome that you may imagine.

Consider the last time you argued with someone to prove your point. Imagine that it was with a child. You proved your point over and over with several examples. Finally, they give in and accept that your point is accurate. You won, right, or did you? When you look into the eyes of the child, you likely see an injured spirit. When humans fight to prove something "right" or "wrong," that energy is as disabling as whatever the conversation was about. You are called to love one another. Love can bear the decision to stop debating your point. Being "right" is about ego and pride. Nothing is gained from breaking another person's spirit simply to prove a point. What benefit is there in being "right" if you damage the relationship as a result?

This is the perfect moment for you to receive another truth: People receive and accept information when they are ready. If a person is unwilling to be open to possibilities, you can pontificate until the cows come home, which will not change their mind. The arguing will change their energy and test their patience. It will not "make" them accept a truth they are not ready to consider.

This dynamic is present as each person decides whether or not they choose to address the places in themselves that require healing. As they make a concerted effort to begin their healing journey, they are likely unaware of the significant impact it will have on others. As evidenced by the example above, the person who can control their responses and stay in a place of peace has achieved personal power. Their agency over themselves helps them build a healthy boundary with others. That boundary is reinforced when they are confronted with triggers like anger and are able to witness it. Observing the emotion, anger, means that they do not take it on or return it to the originator. This is the moment in the example where things change. Healing has helped diffuse the anger by not responding from a wounded state. This is healing.

"What benefit is there in being "right" if you damage the relationship as a result?"

Taking action is all about doing the work to heal. The process is a journey, so many pieces will unfold as they go. It is important to keep doing the work. You will find connections to older/deeper wounds as you heal more recent wounds. You will experience the feeling that you have already addressed the need through healing, only to recognize that there are more pieces to it than you expected.

The example of the iceberg comes back to mind. The part of the iceberg above the water line is more of the new trauma and injury. Underneath the waterline are experiences across the person's lifetime, the impact of ancestral trauma, and the condition of the central soul. Addressing the combination of those things becomes the next step in the healing process. As the need for healing arises that mirrors places you have already addressed, do your best to welcome it. Allow the need to arise and meet it with gratitude. You get to heal this wound at a deeper level. You know how to do it. You recognize the importance of continuing to heal it.

Early on in the journey, you may not want to keep going. You will feel compelled to keep going once you push through to see some results. It is like working out. The first few workouts are filled with enthusiasm. By the second or third week, the apathy of days passed creeps in. The attempts to get you to stop working out create a struggle between the desired results and your desire to stay in the familiar. If you decide to keep going, you will begin to see changes in your physical body. The increase in energy, decrease in stress, and other benefits begin to add additional encouragement to keep going. Momentum is your friend. As you start the journey, commit not to give up. You are worth it, and Healing is required.

Chapter Pearls

- Taking action is about doing the work to heal.

- You cannot convince someone else to heal. Healing is an active choice that requires a willingness to do the work.

Journal Prompts

- What emotions arise as you think about taking action to heal?

- How might you encourage yourself to do the work to heal?

Chapter Ten

Engaging Support

S upport is an integral part of the healing journey. There are many benefits to having support. Accountability is one of the greatest benefits in the early part of your healing journey. Another consideration is the type of expertise that would best support you in the areas you are interested in healing. For example, a trainer is a phenomenal partner when starting an exercise regimen. Suppose you have a history of starting things and not finishing them. In that case, it might be helpful to engage a behavioral coach or select a personal trainer who can support you with designing accountability mechanisms. Often, people will not design the right support system as a result of something that needs healing, like a fear of success. Engaging the right support and being honest about your motivation, previous pitfalls, and fears is critical to your success.

One of the most important things to remember is that the journey to heal is ongoing. Most people need encouragement to keep going. Think about any marathon you have ever seen. Why are there so many people observing throughout the race? They are encouraging the runners to keep going. Often, we see signs calling the person's attention back to their why. The signs, water, supporters, and milestones help the runners feel encouraged as they make the trek.

Healing is similar. People need encouragement and reminders of their why. The challenge is that a roadmap is not as straightforward as you might find in a marathon. Even though the runner knows the entire route and distance, they still need the support available to them. It is clear that healing is a journey, but there is no detailed map or timing that provides a clear path. It makes sense that more support, particularly from those who are gifted at truly seeing others, would show up during the healing journey.

Engaging a coach, advisor, therapist, and whatever else you identify as needed is helpful during your journey. Your work will bring up things that you may not expect, and having someone sort through it will help significantly. Therapists are trained professionals who excel at supporting clients to navigate their journey. Support groups, networks, and spiritual partners are great resources for helping you deepen your learning and can help you accelerate your healing. The benefit of having trusted resources is that they can see what you cannot. For example, financial trauma resources might include a financial planner, therapist, behavioral coach, and spiritual advisor. With each one focused on their expertise, you can begin to address the root behavioral patterns, new beliefs, and a deeper connection to your renewed goals. Remember that if you could see it all from their perspective, you would likely have changed it already. **Most of the time, we under-resource our healing work.**

Imagine a person who enters an emergency room with internal bleeding. They can feel something is wrong, but cannot see it. The physician uses their technology and expertise to create a diagnosis that helps the patient gain understanding around why they feel the way they do. It is identical in healing. In either case, the next step is the patient's decision. They get to choose whether or not to treat the issue and select the course of action. The other powerful thing that happens is the confirmation of what you are experiencing. Support groups, friends, and practitioners alike have experiences that can be relatable. Often, people simply need to hear that they are not alone in what they are navigating and to find confidence in the potential relief that can come from the recommended course of action.

By now, you recognize that much of what is exposed in your healing journey has roots in childhood. That part of life was incredibly formative. You learned to process what was happening in the world through your filter and frame of reference. You also extended an inordinate amount of trust to adults around you, often substituting their beliefs for your own. The inner child healing work I've done has been incredibly beneficial. Going deep with the right practitioner opened up places to explore that brought me deep clarity. I was able to connect with the roots of my patterns of thinking, awareness of why certain triggers create a specific response, and to tap into emotions that needed to be released so that I could finally be free.

In one example, I was preparing to address a childhood trauma by being in the presence of the person who was physically responsible for it. At the same time, I was navigating a relationship issue with my partner. My journey of forgiveness and releasing the trauma occurred years ago, yet there was an unexpected wound that arose. I was working with a therapist and inner child healing coach, and was able to have invaluable time with both to explore what was going on. The self-regulation practices I learned were helping, but I wanted to really understand how these things were tied together and was ready to explore the path to heal whatever arose.

Through the work with my therapist and coach, I connected to some deeply held beliefs about my safety, avoidance, validation, and the trauma that were monumental. Even though I had been working on all of those things over the past few years, the inner child work was what helped me to see the narratives that were the foundation for how I designed my deepest love relationships.

It was so powerful. I was able to finally release some habits that were not supporting my growth in this season of life, and to see how the mechanism that supported me in the past was not aligned with the truth of my experience now. I don't want to minimize the work done in these areas over many years, but the shift I needed happened very quickly. In this instance, within a couple of days of my sessions with my therapist and coach (and some healthy conversations with a family member and a close friend), I was ready to be in the environment. My experience was nothing like what I had been avoiding over the last decade. I was different-centered and clear about what I would contribute to my experience. I did only what was truly comfortable for me, and everything was fine. I know that the support I enlisted made all the difference. I could not have been in that space and at peace without the healing work and support.

God was clearly present as They always are. They also give us nudges about the support we need. A clear prayer for a specific type of therapist, especially her spiritual connectivity and EMDR training, was what I laid before God. Finding her was simple through TherapyforBlackGirls.com. A God connection led me to my inner child healing coach, whose information you can see in the resources at the end of the book. She is amazing. All of the other support people who were there for me in that critical moment were God connections. God also showed me who to talk to and gave me the words to ask for help. My point to you is this: sometimes we don't ask for help because we think, "I gave it to God and therefore it will just get fixed." I asked God for help and to clarify what part of the work was mine to do. I was open to the idea that support might need to be more than one person, like when a medical team confers on a complex case. If you really want to heal, assemble the support you need.

As a practitioner, I know what God shows me for people. I see their purpose, and God speaks to me about the things that would benefit them on their journey. For my business and advisory clients, I do not represent myself as a one-stop solution. I have a distinct role to play, and there are other experts who are meant to support them as well. My work is to guide and advise. It is accelerated when they have a strong team around them, the right board, and the support of experts who can triage a specific issue or concern. The right support is an investment that leads to a significant impact that would likely take years to address on your own.

Those who enjoy journaling will find that a healing journal will help them track their journey and capture progress. It can help you identify cycles and trends that will provide valuable data for you and anyone you engage with in your journey. You measure what matters. That is a valid truth across all areas of your healing journey. Your journal will help you see your growth in real time, and it will help you develop comfort in standing in your truth. It also helps you formulate the words you need to speak your truth to yourself and others. If you have kept a journal while reading this book, you have likely found it beneficial to review your thoughts as you progressed through the prompts. It was intended to show you the benefit of journaling when you are in the moment.

If you choose to journal, you may now use it as a guide to identify some of the places you may want to heal. Simply asking the question, "Why did that truth impact me in that way?" will open doors for you. Those doors lead to places that can be explored and will help you examine whether or not healing is required there. Enjoy the process.

This would be an excellent time to journal about the ways that you want to explore healing for yourself. What modalities interested you most? Were you surprised that so many recommendations support all areas of healing? What might you choose that could help you across all four, and which practices will help you focus more deeply on a specific body?

Chapter Pearls

- Accountability and encouragement are important when you begin healing work. Identifying the right resources is equivalent to having the right Rx for your ailment. Knowing the areas you want to prioritize will help you identify the type of support that you will need.

- Engaging support is a gift that you give to yourself. Imagine that your healing journey is like training to run a marathon. Hiring a coach or utilizing a system will help you create the right infrastructure to ensure that you train well.

- The memories, thoughts, and ideas that arise as you read

provide a roadmap for your healing. Give yourself quiet time to process them as they arise. Capture as much as you can in your journal. These pages in your journal will be filled with precious gems of light to help guide you on the journey to heal.

Journal Prompts

- Reflect on what you have experienced as you have read this book. What revelations of self came up for you? How did you feel as you faced some of your thoughts or patterns?

- Make a list of the resources and support that you believe you will need for your journey. Identify the ones that will help you feel the most confident about taking action today to begin your healing journey. What commitment are you making to find and engage that support? When will you begin? What other steps are required? Write down the actionable steps and your plan to follow up.

Chapter Eleven

Your Body Can Heal

A lign with the idea that the body is composed of physical, mental, emotional, and spiritual elements or "bodies." Each has a role in your healing experience and needs to be explored and supported by healing. There is ongoing maintenance and, of course, additional healing as you prepare for the next levels in your journey.

One consideration that may support your understanding of healing is remembering when key events happened in your life. Therapists often ask their clients, "When was the first time you can remember feeling or experiencing this emotion or event?" The patient begins to work backward in their mind to find the first time that they can consciously remember. Hypnotherapists have noted that often, their clients will identify experiences that happened in a lifetime before this existence.

Regardless of the starting point for the experience, it is reasonable to believe that there are layers one must pass through to remember when things "began." If it is reasonable to believe that there are layers that we must go through to recall the impetus for how we feel, behave, and react, as examples, then we can apply the same thinking to our healing journey.

Healing happens in layers. As each layer is healed, there is a process of settling into the feeling of the layer. As the next layer is revealed, a deeper level of healing occurs. The pace of healing each layer is determined by the individual, with the understanding that each part must heal. As you begin to explore the actions you can take to heal yourself, hold a concept around "creating environments." When you create a toxic environment, the living beings placed in that space will suffer and likely take on the traits of the environment. Create a healthy environment, and you have done what you can to support the beings in their ability to thrive. The environments created in your body have an impact on your experience. It touches on a broad range of elements, including mindset, physical conditioning, emotional responsiveness, and spiritual connectedness. These are just some of the examples of elements within your reach that can help you create conditions to help you heal, grow, and thrive.

As you begin or continue in your healing journey, it is important to see yourself in a different role than what you may have chosen before. Earlier, we discussed your role as the COO of your life. As the head of your composed healing team, you can now see yourself as the Chief Healing Officer as well. In your role, you design the right team and select the right people to fill the positions. This team will help you on your healing journey. You may feel that you do not have the expertise to lead the charge, but be assured that you do. There is no other person in the world who has the capacity to care more about your full healing than you do. Others may carry specialization and expertise, or they may be a loved one who cares very deeply for you, but they cannot truly match the depth of desire you have to heal yourself.

You must start with choice. You get to decide if you want to heal fully. When the decision to heal fully is made, you can begin by identifying where to start. Healing fully is an ongoing journey, so the decision is affirmed by the subsequent choices that make up the path to healing. Understanding what you want to address first will help you select the right team (support) to help you heal.

Imagine the boardroom table filled with the right support team you hand-selected. You have brought them into this private space. You sit at the head of the table, sharing the details that only you know about your journey. The articulation of your highest vision of healing across mind, body, and spirit is described in detail to your team. The impending dialogue creates a beautiful sharing of information, ideas, protocols, and questions; all focused on supporting you in becoming the healed person you know is within. You choose the next steps and design the plan with your confidants. Your Source is present and illuminating the path to healing. You take a deep breath and begin the journey, knowing that in time, you will heal the beautiful layers as you continue the precious journey of your life. Each layer will unfold with lessons and insights that meld beautifully into the gifts you are intended to give to the world. Yes, this is your unique journey, and you deserve the healing, peace, joy, and love along the way.

To effectively support the larger goals of healing, the CHO, you, will have to create clarity and connections for your healing support team. All too often, providers are given too little information. The mindset shift and recognition that you have more information than you realize is always true. A decision must be made to lead the healing work, knowing that you can connect with your body- physically, mentally, emotionally, and spiritually to know what is needed. Worry less about the how and allow yourself first to become grounded in the knowledge that this is what is needed, and you will have more answers than you could imagine.

You enlist your team in your journey by sharing your experiences and conditions. While it may feel a bit arduous initially, there is no greater feeling. Most practitioners are great at what they do and are incredibly purpose-driven. Often, many will spend hours thinking about solutions, even researching and praying for answers on how best to support clients in complex cases. There are stories of doctors reaching out worldwide through forums, networks, and referrals to find information to support complex cases. Ongoing gratitude is deserved for that level of demonstrated care and love.

At the same time, you are the only one who lives with the culmination of all that you are each and every day. It is time for you to take on the role of number one advocate and raise the level of accountability for all areas of your health, wellness, and healing.

As you address areas in one part of the body, you will experience shifts in other areas. Addressing a physical ailment may bring forth a wave of emotions or reveal another area of healing required for the body. Understand that healing is a beautiful process, yet it is not without challenge and change. The blessing for you is that you can readily choose peace and ease on the other side of the work.

Physical Body

You already know a lot about healing the physical body. You have experienced band-aids and medication and may have had some exposure to specialized treatments like orthopedics or minor surgeries.

Some common experiences come to mind about healing the physical body. Much of what is taught is based on responding to conditions rather than the proactive ways that you can care for your body. Healing the physical body qualifies as responsive to current conditions and preventative for future conditions.

When you heal the body, you will address underlying conditions that create environments for dis-ease to thrive. Physical healing is a very broad topic, as the body comprises eleven major organ systems. The process of addressing physical conditions is relative to the area being addressed. Each condition can benefit from the expertise of a specialist, the constant care of your general practitioner, a nutritionist, and a therapist. Physical therapists, personal trainers, and coaches are also great resources as you work to heal these areas.

It may surprise you to see the recommended list includes a therapist. As you make adjustments to your physical body, you will experience emotional shifts. Your mindset must change as you work on your physical self. The support of the psychological and emotional practitioners is critical to help through the entire journey. After all, this is transformative work. The roots of the unhealed conditions are not always readily seen, so support in processing what you are experiencing is paramount.

As you begin the work to heal your physical body, as with all parts, you should begin with a vision of the change you want to see. Capturing images in your mind, descriptions in your journal, pictures, etc., helps you to make it real. Sit each day with the vision of what you want. What will it feel like to be relieved of the root cause and symptoms? How will you experience life differently? This works with internal and external conditions. See it and know that it can change. Command your body to align with the change. Deepen your belief every day and open yourself up to the possibility that healing will happen miraculously.

Over time, you will gain comfort in this new state of being you are creating for yourself. You must see it over and over again in your mind for it to be so. Daily meditation is a great tool. As you gain comfort in your vision, begin to look inside your body or to the root of the disease. If it is eczema, you may see the condition sitting on the surface of the skin. The root is within the body, and triggers are vast. Quiet time may help you identify what is happening within. One of the most beautiful gifts you can give to your body is the time to listen to what it has to say and then to trust your knowledge. There is something behind what you feel in your body; sometimes, people stop exploring before they make the connections.

There is a wide range of ways to take care of the physical body and to create the conditions for healing. Most are complementary and produce excellent outcomes when combined. Keep in mind that your choices should be aligned with your current state and the improvements you want to make. Healing is a journey. Treat the body with incredible love and respect as you engage it in your healing work.

As always, you should listen to your body and discuss new practices with your choice of practitioners. Movement is critical and requires a plan and appropriate monitoring by a practitioner, especially when starting a new regimen. Healing is about taking care of yourself. You are the goal, and your healing is the accurate measure of progress.

- Rest and good sleep hygiene

- Movement and Exercise (daily- walking

- Grounding/ Earthing (see notes)

- Diagnostics

- Nutrition and dietary changes (increased organic fresh fruit and vegetables)

- Cleansing

- Homeopathic remedies and plant medicine

- Acupuncture and Acupressure

- Lymphatic Massage

- Rebounder

- Somatic Stretching

- Massage

- Cold Plunge

- Sauna

- Herbal Teas and Tinctures

- Regular elimination and good digestive practices

These are some things to consider as you think about healing your physical body. In general, movement, the right food choices, elimination, and rest are a great start. In many cases, committing to address gaps in self-care puts an individual right on the path to healing. There may be some ideas on the list that you are unfamiliar with. Exploring new options can be a pathway to your healing. Providing new stimuli and honoring your response to the experience affirms connectedness to your body and relaxes the brain's automatic response. Curiosity and exploration are generally excellent conditions for encouraging healing. They support the expansion of your current perspective.

Emotional Body

The emotional body houses critical information for healing. Healing begins with exploring our relationship to the emotions we experience. The question "how do you really feel?" can be fully loaded. Perhaps you may not be sure how you feel, or you may experience an avalanche of emotions as you attempt to answer that question. It is ok. All is well. Emotions are often repressed or even expressed under the cover of a less complex emotion. For example, fear is often masked by an angry or frustrated response. As previously mentioned, love can be stifled by avoiding possible rejection.

It is not a simple matter. Emotions are deeply connected to our experiences and the meaning-making part of our minds. They can be stored in our tissue at a cellular level. This often presents itself as a physical condition. Knots in the stomach are a familiar reference. The knots are connected to the emotional brain that is within the gut. Imagine the gut being full of words left unsaid, intuition ignored, and emotions that were "swallowed" and unable to be processed. That presents as physical and emotional tension within the body. The mind also begins to create a new story as a response to unaddressed emotions. Healthy expression of emotions is key to creating a remarkable life. First, one chooses to experience the emotions and learns to do so without judgment. They recognize emotions as messengers. Emotions help us to build bridges between experiences and the mind. There is a choice available to receive the emotion as is, without falling into a pattern of self-deprecation for having the feeling arise. As healing occurs, it becomes more evident that emotions are a critical part of self-care and self-love.

What if you did not need to hide your emotions or hide from them? How might it free you to allow the emotion to be experienced and accepted without judgment? Could experiencing your emotions become a gift rather than a burden? Of course. Joy, happiness, excitement, surprise, love, and peace are all emotions. The connotation we attach helps us see them as a gift based on the meaning that we have made from it. The meaning we make from fear, anger, resentment, and other emotions characterized as unfavorable is often connected to avoidance. The emotions are not actions; they are feelings. It is what you choose to do that creates the meaning.

Fear by itself simply notifies you that there is a condition present that you should be aware of. It may also encourage a desire for safety or protection. The feeling is not what created the condition or the response to it. When the environment and the reaction or response are seen clearly as the pieces to explore, we can let go of much of the grief created over the years around emotions. Emotional healing begins with releasing meaning and being curious about what emotions desire to teach us. Examining patterns and triggers is a beautiful way to support emotional healing.

- Accept emotions without judgment

- Journaling

- Mindfulness

- Curiosity and inquiry

- Therapy and Coaching

- EMDR

- Somatic Healing

- Speak freely

- Neuroplasticity Exercises

- Rest and Sleep Hygiene

- Movement and exercise

- Build healthy relationships

Psychological Body

The mind is incredibly powerful. It creates what you see as reality on an ongoing basis. Without directing it, your mind will direct you. In innocence, this is less of a risk. As you age, the reverse is true. The more you experience, the more confirmation the mind has to determine what is acceptable in your life. It is diligent and excellent at its job-safety, continuity, lower risk, and preserving energy through making regular activities autonomous.

Days are filled with automatic choices and decisions based on the past. While it is good to spend energy on higher activities than repetitive choices, without clear intentions, the mind is left unchecked.

A deeper look reveals to us that there is even more to understand about the mind-body connection. The mind regulates behavior as well, and it creates meaning in the world around you. The way you see things is filtered through your mind. The filter is clouded when a person operates from an unhealed state (without actively healing and bringing thought to the ongoing processes in the mind). It is easy to experience the world in an impure way because of the condition of the filter. The way the world operates becomes a prism, creating complexity and confusion for this incredible organ that wants to process and simplify things for the individual.

The heart is considered to be erratic, as it is the place where feelings emerge. Imagine that the heart is constantly moving based on emotional responses to what is going on around you, and the brain is moving methodically through the templates that it has created. Of course, the tendency to trust logic and familiarity emerges. The problem is that the heart is working through the lens of things that have occurred. It looks irrational and unstable compared to the brain, but which is true?

The heart desperately points back to the truth within. What can look chaotic is actually a process of calling you back to your truth. It encourages you to explore within and to address the unhealed places, even though the heart knows that more emotions will emerge to be healed. Turning our attention back to the brain brings us the realization that the beauty of how the brain works in this typically more logical fashion precludes us from always seeking the truth within.

One is not better than the other, per se. They both have important roles to play, but the order in which we seek leadership has to change until the filter of the mind has been cleared and operates in concert with the life created by your higher self with the Divine.

Taking action to heal psychologically requires an evaluation of the paradigms that you live by. So much of what needs to be explored has become commonplace and regular in the way that you operate that it is likely difficult to see. You can change your mindset, heal mental health conditions, and retrain your brain by yourself. It is absolutely possible, and there are numerous examples of people who have done it. In most cases, they have been spirit-led, and their desire for change was at an incredible high; it was as if there were only one option... to change or else.

For most, you will find that support to address the mind, behaviors, and patterns that make up the psychological body works best. The great news is that there are countless ways to address the work and to create transformative change. Consider an approach that offers expert practitioners and community support to encourage you as you do this work. In addition, a daily singular practice will be highly beneficial to all people.

That might be prayer, meditation, journaling, or an energetic practice with a mind-body connection like Qi Gong or Yoga to supplement the work you do with support from others.

The most important thing to remember is that your mind is doing its job. It makes sense of what is available to it. Consider that it has done its job to bring you to this moment, and with the intention of protecting you, it has created multiple ways to keep you safe. It is effective.

Remember that as an individual, you have gone through so many experiences that have brought you to this moment. There is not a single textbook approach that is equally effective for everyone. You are unique. This moment in your journey requires a protocol that is fitting for you.

Explore and incorporate the recommendations below into your plan. This is the moment you get to align it with a new, clear agenda that you are setting. This agenda aligns with spirit to bring all of you to an integrated way of living and growing. Give yourself a lot of grace as you journey through healing your mindset and psychological conditioning.

- Therapy and counseling

- Hypnotherapy

- Meditation, Guided Imagery

- Energy work

- EMDR

- Supplements

- Homeopathic support

- Nutrition

- Stress and anxiety management

- Breathwork

- Brain retraining Exercises

- Walking and moderate exercise (>15-20 mins resets the Limbic system.

- Neuroplasticity Practices- NLP, Somatic Expression

- Sleep

- Healing communities and support groups

Spiritual Body

Healing yourself spiritually brings all of the parts together. Spiritual healing is about realignment. The process of healing helps you confront narratives that are limiting and typically scarcity-based. As a divine being, you are abundant, just as your Creator is the Source of all abundance. Spirituality is a journey of seeking truth. For the individual, one asks, what is my truth? The healing journey is a blur of reconnecting to your inner child and higher self. These are genuine parts of you that hold information about your truth. To navigate this life, you have made choices and responded to circumstances beyond your control that are a part of the disconnect from the inner self. This is a part of life. The journey is about remembering who you are, rediscovering your purpose, and making choices that will support you in becoming who you choose to be.

Before you were born, there was a purpose created with you. You sat with God and designed the journey for this life. It is ok that you may not remember the pathway or choices. There is a map within, and through your healing work, you can rediscover it. You can also seek God for the answers. They will emerge as you continue to heal. Bravery is a part of spiritual self-healing. You will experience your bravery during the journey; you don't have to see yourself as brave at the onset. In time, you will be able to witness all that you have overcome and see yourself so differently. It is a precious part of this healing work.

Consider spirituality as your life's compass. When you are walking due north, you can go in that direction for a long time without having to check back to ensure that you are still on track. That is what the compass of spirituality is like. You know directionally where you are going. As you heal spiritually, you begin to understand what it feels like to be on the path to a more specific destination. There is flexibility about how you get there and when, but you have clarity about the what. Most importantly, the person that you are comes into focus more and more.

Within you is your purpose. It is a part of the way that you connect with humanity and with the Divine. The connection to something greater than yourself is a part of the pathway to more in your life. Healing on this level creates answers to so many questions you have carried in your life. As you heal the other areas of the body, healing in the spirit adds clarity to why the other parts of your journey matter, and you will begin to have peace with how it will be used in concert with the journey ahead.

One of the best ways to look at healing this part of the body is an exploration of who you are at your core. We are all spirit first, and through the birthing process, we become human beings. Connecting our spirit to the journey of life creates meaning and helps us to release paradigms that block us from operating in love.

As you embark on this part of your healing journey, remember that this is about seeking the truth within. Time to yourself exploring your beliefs, reconnecting to your intuition or inner voice, and connecting to God is at the center of what you are healing. There are many ways to support spiritual healing, but it is important to remember that the foundation of the relationship is between you and God first, and then your relationship with yourself.

Religion and spirituality are distinct concepts. Many find it challenging to grasp a sense of spiritual connectedness that is not grounded in religion. At this moment, you are invited to release that notion. Spirituality forms the foundation that allows religion to exist and connect with inner truths. While religion can be inherently beautiful, it lacks depth without an individual's spirituality. It is the spiritual connection that breathes life into any religious practice.

This is important to note as you begin the work. Your connection or religious practices cannot replace your spiritual connectedness. The opposite is true. The more deeply you are connected spiritually, the more your religious practices and beliefs can serve the highest good for mankind. Often, people trade religious practices for their spiritual compass. That is a circuitous route; it will always eventually lead you back to the question that you first need to answer for yourself.

While there are many supportive practices and practitioners to support this healing, the critical relationship is that of you and yourself. A wonderful benefit of healing is that because it all works well together, your spiritual healing will begin to lead you forward on a path of alignment, intention, and personal truth. Your sovereignty, oneness with self, and alignment with the divine are required to make the full impact you are here to make.

- Daily Prayer and Meditation

- Guided Imagery

- Visualization

- Intuitive practices and healing)

- Spiritual Coaching (life coaching and other coaching modalities as well)

- Energy work (past life regression, DNA activation, Reiki)

- Qi Gong

- Faith-based support groups and communities

- Religious practices- worship, prayer, and services

- Journaling

- Transformational development programs and courses

- Reading daily

- Sound healing and music

- Plant medicine

- Travel and exploration of new places

- Spiritual and religious writings (Bible, Quran/Koran, Torah, Tripitaka, Bhagavad Gita or Mahabharata, and I Ching are a limited list of examples)

- Therapy and counseling

- Creative experiences and hobbies that encourage self-exploration.

- Rest and Sleep Hygiene

Chapter Pearls

- Healing happens in layers. Each layer revealed is an opportunity to witness yourself and to choose to continue the healing process. The journey is designed to be at a pace with your desire and readiness to heal. Set your mind on creating the journey to be what you need as an individual, rather than comparing your process to that of others.

- You are the CHO, Chief Healing Officer, of your life. This is an active role, requiring you to chart the path to heal. Selecting the team, tools, and process is a part of your assignment.

Journal Prompts

- Each of the bodies has healing needs. Many of the ways you can support healing overlap with the other bodies. For example, therapy can address all areas of the body in varied ways. Reflect on healing modalities or practices that could support you in two or more areas. Which resources and practitioners might support you with a multi-pronged approach?

- Some of the resources may be unfamiliar to you. Which ones are most intriguing? What interests you most? Choose one and identify what you would want to work through using that resource? Journal about the choices you are making to expose yourself to this resource during your healing journey.

- Reflect on any biases that you noted about various practices. Where is the origin of those thoughts or beliefs? What can exploring the root help you discern about your truth?

- Your purpose is the way you connect to the divine and is an integral part of your healing. Journal about what you understand your purpose to be at this time (remembering that purpose unfolds over time). How do you see your healing unlocking more of your connection to your purpose? What choices will you make today to bring more of your purpose work into your reasons why healing is required?

Chapter Twelve

You Can Heal With God's Help

No matter the journey or what you may have tried before, you can heal with God's help. God remains the CEO of your life. You are the COO of your life and have now taken on the CHO- Chief Healing Officer role. If you reflect back on the practice of assembling the support team, you will recall that you sat at the head of the table. Most of the practices outlined in this book can be completed without the intentional inclusion of God. As the CHO, you get to decide who sits at the table to work on the healing of the person God created.

Remember that all healing comes from God. There is a difference in actively including God in your healing journey. Seek God. Invite God. You want God in the room. God, the source of all, who designed you and knows every part of you. The same God created a purpose for you and established the choices and optimum experiences for you in this life. Of course, there is a choice to plow forward without God, but ask yourself why you would want that. How could that ever be in your best interest?

Experts are welcome in any situation where something needs to be repaired. In most cases, people would choose an electrician for electrical work and a neurologist for brain surgery. Both are excellent with their hands, have incredibly detailed technical/medical knowledge, and have the experience to problem-solve well. Neither would be welcome to do the work in the other's field without having learned and applied knowledge.

In the same way, you can convene experts to support you in improving your life through healing, but God holds parts of the master plan that you do not remember yet or cannot see. When you connect with experts and the team, make sure you create space for God to be in the room. If there is an aversion to the inclusion of God, you are encouraged to ask yourself this. "Is it God that I am unsure of, or is it me? Is it what I have been told? Is it my reaction to experiences? Where and when did I begin to feel a disconnect with how welcome God is in my life?"

Whatever your answer is, honor it. So much of what has been taught makes people feel shameful for questioning God or feeling disconnected. What if this moment of conflict is exactly what you need to begin seeking again? Often, people, in their limited perspective, have painted pictures of God that are misaligned with what they know to be true or hold as a distant memory from before they were born. God is incredibly more expansive than what most people understand and are willing to accept. Recognizing who God truly is and the co-creation of this life's journey with you is critical for your evolution. Your growth will reveal the real proximity to God, and your acceptance of that will change your life forever.

This really is the first place where healing is required. What if you accepted at this moment that there is more for you to learn about God and more that you want God to reveal to you about who you are? The simple acceptance of that statement as your truth puts you on the way to building an intimate relationship with God that can quite literally change your life.

Allowing God to help you heal is transformative. God is the foundation of all things, so in essence, God is always there. God is present within you in the ways that you will allow. Likening it to having access to a fully detailed blueprint for building a house from the ground up, but you'd rather choose to build it from your memory, basing it on what your childhood home looked like. Even a person with the best memory cannot identify every step, and certainly not in order. Most people would readily accept the blueprint and choose to remember that they can make modifications as they go *because the house is theirs.*

God desires to be desired by you. God wants to be included in your healing journey. They want to have an intimate relationship with you. They want to be your safe place and to help you love yourself even more than you already do. They desire to see you fulfill everything you came here to do. They know your role in helping heal the world and are always ready to help you along the path. This is the truth, God's truth. God wants you to know that Healing Is Required and that They want to be your chosen partner on the journey.

Chapter Pearls

- God desires to be your active partner in your healing journey.

- Allowing God to help you heal is transformative.

Journal Prompts

- In what ways will you seek God and invite Them into your healing work?

- What do you know to be true in your soul about who God is to you? How might you let go of what you have been taught to embrace a more personal and intimate relationship with God?

Postlude

Who were you before the world told you who you were? That is the question we answer during this journey of life. Healing is about reconnecting you with this truth. Can you remember the things that you loved to do as a child? What did you want to be? What things did and perhaps still do set your soul on fire? If you need any proof that God deposited something special within you, answering these questions should suffice.

This is the moment the next stage in your healing begins. You have begun to see yourself and to remember. You know why your healing matters to you, to humanity, and God. You know why you matter to you, to humanity, and God. You are a precious part of the puzzle, and your Healing is required.

There is nothing like living the life you were created to experience. If you have been feeling disconnected lately, know that this is why. The more time goes on, the more pronounced the disconnect is. The more long-term, for clarity of purpose, and to see ourselves creating an impact. Healing can be a part of the legacy you leave for your family and humanity. Everything you do to heal creates a leg up for the generations to follow. Do your healing work. They deserve to experience a world that is better than it was when you found it.

For many, focusing on others has always been a more natural choice. Allow this moment of truth to sink in. Taking care of others can be beautiful when you have enough to share and are pouring from a pure place. Often, we take care of others to hide how we feel about ourselves. The feeling of being unworthy or simply fearful of what is to come hinders us from taking care of ourselves. The best way you can care for others is by first taking care of yourself. It is also true that resentment sets in when we pour all we have into others and find ourselves depleted. It is also true that your breakthrough opens doors of possibilities for others. Over time, we become exhausted by the cycle, resulting in our not wanting to take care of ourselves or others.

> Healing can be a part of the legacy you leave for your family and humanity.
>
> — Anika Apple

It will become more natural for you to prioritize your healing once you begin. Many of the ideas represented in the book that you have an aversion to will shift. It is ok. In the current state, you can only see with the current filter. As the filter expands, you will have more space for possibilities. Possibilities will change things. Your perspective will change everything. As a result, you will emerge as the beautiful butterfly who has had a lovely yet arduous journey as a caterpillar. Have you ever considered that because the caterpillar moves along slowly, it has a relationship with its own resilience, giving it the confidence that it can make it through the stages of the transformation to become a butterfly? It knows its purpose, trusts the past, and focuses on what is required in the present moment. It is so similar to this moment in your life. I hope you choose to form your wings, too.

The Path to Healing

As you read this book, I hope that it is evident to you that these words are not my own. This book was divinely delivered by God and included direction to me about which stories to share. I found myself flooded with memories at times when I needed to pause to explore my own healing. Some of what I aptly coined were moments where my own healing took center stage. As I returned to the book to write and during the editing process, I recognized that the delays were actually moments for more revelation that was needed for the book.

It is an honor to have been chosen to birth this book and to support humanity on a path to healing. We need it.

I began this book in 2022, writing the majority of it by the end of June in 2023. I remember wondering why I needed to hit this timeline and then watch the book sit on my computer for what felt like forever. God had given me a timeline that I did not understand. Over time, there would be beautiful insights God would share, many that I thought should go right into the book. God did not direct me to add them. It felt like I was collecting thoughts and information for the book that would never make it in.

In August of 2023, God revealed that it was time to create a community that would focus on providing guidance and support for people during their healing journey. The Healing Crusade was born. It was the culmination of multiple prophetic words given to me over time and some downloads that God had released, which I had no idea what to do with. In 2021, I met someone who, in our first conversation, told me I would "Heal the world." I was blown away because God had said those exact words to me a few months prior. I had not shared it with anyone. Over time, I continued to ask God my favorite question at the time: "How?" I've learned that the answer to "how" belongs to God and that I am supposed to focus on my part. That August, God spoke through another prophetic voice and confirmed the building of the healing container that is The Healing Crusade.

I spent a few weeks seeking God for clarity, and the vision was incredible. We would build the largest active online healing community in the world. God called the Healing Crusade "A Container of Miracles" and gave me specific clarity on how to design each section. A few months later, we would open the doors, and many of my inner circle chose to be founding members. Since its inception, we have been iterating and learning how to create a community. What we know for sure is that Healing is required and that we will have what we believe is possible.

On the day that I launched the first invitation-only info session, there was a miracle. By the end of 4 days, we had three miracles that occurred. God was clearly showing us that prayers were being answered as we walked in faith. What I did not expect was a journey that would continue to have me healing actively and publicly in the way that it has. I know that the first part of this journey has been about me, my team, and the inner circle's healing before expanding into what God showed me about this community. The path is being led by God, and we are following without knowing all of the steps.

God reminds me regularly to remind the Crusaders that their faith is required to see miracles. We have a member who just received a double lung transplant. She joined while on the list for the transplant and spent the better part of 6 months in the hospital waiting for her surgery. We prayed for and with her. She came believing in her miracle, and we have seen God move in her life! Glory to God. There have been other prayers answered, connections and purpose revealed in the community, and we are healing in accordance with our commitment to doing the work. God answered my prayers as well.

A couple of months after the community was established, my mother was diagnosed with Breast Cancer. She is now a survivor and has finished both chemotherapy and radiation. I remember the range of emotions that I had with God, complete with my weeping and yelling at God that this was not our agreement. I had very clearly told God that I would do all that God asked of me and asked that my children and parents be protected, healthy, and have long lives. I was furious about her diagnosis. I even threw my hand warmer against the wall and smashed it in a very uncharacteristic fashion. My son came to check on me and found me weeping and began to repair the hand warmer. He held my hands as I told him about his grandmother's diagnosis. He looked at me, and his heart seemed to say, "But Mom, you know who God is."

Yes, I do know who God is. The very one who took me on my own healing journey and has taught me to see the world differently. The same God who designed this healing container and answered my many prayers, often with visible miracles. The community was in place for my mother and others to have what they needed in terms of support for their healing journey, and I needed it as well. A few days before an appointment she had scheduled, God instructed us to fast and pray with specificity about the outcome we wanted. I will never forget our conversation that Saturday morning. She woke up and could no longer feel the lump. It shrunk! There was no other explanation but God. The radiologist and specialist had an extremely difficult time finding the lump on the scans later that day. My mom was sure that God had her, and so was I. The rest of the story is hers to tell, but I will say this: I will never doubt that The Healing Crusade is a container of miracles.

We built it to do what it has done in the way that God directed. The process is a beautiful mix of ongoing challenges and weekly focus areas to help you heal while creating the space for you to explore your healing at your own pace. The community element is present for people to have what they need, and we know that it will evolve as the needs of the members evolve, just as God planned. We built it for you, for my family, and for God. We will heal the world alongside the army of light-carrying, love-wielding healers that God created for this work. I hope you know, dear friend, you are not alone. We are here, crusading forward, bringing God's love and miracles to all who are open to seeing. You are not alone.

By now, you know that you will need support on your journey. As I shared throughout the book, my own healing has been amplified by the proximity of others, communities, and direct work with experts who constantly help me to unlock the next level of growth. God clearly shows me myself, and even with my divine understanding of healing, I still need others. You deserve to have people around you who are committed to healing and growth. You deserve to be seen and supported. I hope you will choose to allow others to witness your growth as a source of inspiration for themselves as well.

Your Path to Healing

I am genuinely grateful that you chose to read this book. I believe the rest of the world is thankful as well. You have decisions ahead about what and how you will choose to continue healing. You have also experienced healing as you read the book, especially in the moments that felt controversial for you. Remember that it takes time to see your progress and experience your healing. Imagine walking on an outdoor track. At the moment, you are focused on the next step. When you turn your head to look behind you, you can appreciate the distance you have traveled from the starting point. It is the same with healing. You get to choose to heal and know that you are making progress, even if your current environment feels similar.

Take your time to connect to what you need as you design your healing path. Learn to listen to your body and Spirit as you do the work. Rest often and extend grace to yourself always. You are doing the best that you can, even when your thinking mind presents you with a list of all of the ways things could be different. Sometimes, we are simply not ready to do more because we need to witness what is within us that desires to be seen.

Share your healing journey. Imagine if your elders shared all of their experiences, conditions, and patterns with you. That information is priceless. You can accelerate understanding through conversation. Talk about the things that you are healing. Allow your community and family to support you and witness your journey. Name what you are experiencing so that others can connect it to their own patterns and choices. There is far too much wisdom within us, both known and continuously revealed, to keep it to ourselves. We are meant to share it with one another.

I hope that you and your method of noticing & notating become rhythmic like your breath. Journaling in any form will provide immense value to you. It is one of the best ways to chronicle your journey and capture the pivotal decisions that open the doors to your healing. It also reinforces the message of how important you are to yourself. What you capture in your journal is information on many levels. It is a place to witness your own growth, patterns, and contains a beautiful way to see yourself. Consider it as a treasure map as you close the last page. In that journal is buried treasure that you can retrieve whenever you need it. You deserve to be seen, and seeing yourself fully is an incredible gift.

My Facilitation/ My role

My assignment is to help us heal. It is to bring God's light into spaces so people experience the love of God and remember that they can access the healing they need. In my current practice, I support the transformation of people into the change catalysts they were created to be. I reconnect people to their purpose in order to become the vessels of divine impact that God created. That work spreads across AAPEX, my signature advisory solution, Integration Coaching, and the courses and programs I lead. I offer divine guidance sessions that support individuals in reconnecting to themselves (intuition), to God, and to transitioned loved ones. My work is recalibration to self and the divine. I am here to raise the frequency of love on the earth, support healing, and elevate our understanding of truth as God delivers it. Wherever you are in your journey, I hope that this book has exceeded your expectations, and when you are ready for more, I will be here.

Peace and Blessings,

Learn More at AnikaApple.com/blog